Air Warfare

THE FOURTH GENERATION

Air
Warfare

THE FOURTH GENERATION

Christy
Campbell

Hamlyn

Designed by Grahame Dudley
Illustrations: Hayward Art Group

First published in 1984 by
The Hamlyn Publishing Group Limited
London · New York · Sydney · Toronto
Astronaut House, Feltham, Middlesex,
England

ISBN 0 600 38523 X
Printed in Italy

Contents

Introduction

At the outset of the 1980s the US Air Force commissioned a study called *Air Force 2000: Air Power Entering the 21st Century*. It drew a broad picture of the world in which air power would operate, before looking at the challenges and opportunities that new technology would open up.

The pattern of US-Soviet superpower confrontation would, it thought, still be set solid but overpopulation, global food and energy shortages, together with the possession of nuclear weapons by emerging powers, would produce new challenges. Western Europe would remain the main security concern of the United States, but new Soviet-backed threats would have to be confronted in the Middle East and elsewhere. All this would require restructured forces and aircraft capable of long-range intervention. It concluded: 'The possibility of a peaceful global environment in the future seems remote'.

Such studies may make disturbing reading for those who are not military-minded because of their apparent assumption that conflict is inevitable and imminent. This, however, is the paradoxical role of military practitioners—whoever they may be—constantly to assume that the worst is going to happen, that it is going to happen today, and to keep one's forces in the highest state of readiness in order to meet it.

The very large numbers of highly sophisticated and expensive combat aircraft in Europe on both sides, for example, have grown rather than diminished in military significance in the age of the intercontinental ballistic missile, because it is the ability to meet a conventional attack, at whatever level of violence it is made, that is the cornerstone of NATO's nuclear deterrent policy.

Similarly, the build-up of highly capable deep-ranging conventional air power by the Soviet Union during the 1970s, in parallel with strategic rocket forces matching the long-range missile arsenal of the United States, has delivered a far greater range of policy options, allowing global challenges which were impossible in the early days of crude nuclear blackmail.

This paradox is joined by another—the actions and capabilities of the perceived opponent are not necessarily the direct imperatives for action. This is because technology has a dynamic all of its own. If technology delivers a new capability that renders existing equipment second-best—behind the 'state of the art'—then combat aircraft need not be consumed in battle. They move gently towards the boneyard on their own account.

In spite of a popular conception that the rate of technological change is speeding up, in a sense the reverse is true. The technology of combat aircraft, for example, concentrates in a single system enormous economic and research resources which might previously have been spread over a much wider range of projects. Development times, on the other hand, stretch beyond service life and run into scores of years. The Tornado, for example, flew in prototype form nearly ten years before it entered service and it will still be a front-line aircraft in the next century. If the B-52 stays in service until then, which seems likely, its 50-year life span will be the equivalent of World War I biplanes turning up in the Vietnam War.

While aircraft designed in the last two decades, such as the Tornado, the F-16 and F-15, will remain familiar shapes in the sky for many years to come, the revolution in information technology is set to alter radically the shape of combat aircraft. Information technology is concerned with the handling of very large amounts of data in a very short time and expressing them as models made up of numbers. For example, a pilot flying a traditional aircraft gives commands through the control surfaces to alter the attitude and direction of the aircraft he is flying. Otherwise it will fly in the direction in which it is pointing. If he could give 100 commands a second he could constantly 'fly' a highly manoeuvrable but inherently unstable airframe, which would otherwise fall out of the sky. Obviously the human brain cannot do it but a computerized fly-by-wire flight control system can. Thus, miniaturized computer power is making possible 'controlled configuration vehicle' airframe technology, the kind of shape seen in the joint-European fighter programme agile combat aircraft, the Israeli Lavi, the Swedish Gripen and the US AFTI demonstrator.

The position with weapon system technology is similar. Current medium-range missiles require the constant illumination of the target by the launch aircraft's radar to be able to home in on the received reflections. Computer technology allows the next generation to be given, prior to launch, a digital model of the place in the sky where the target will be, before homing with its own miniaturized active radar—making it a true 'fire-and-forget system'.

Voice-command cockpits are already in prototype form and systems have been tested which cut into the pilot's decision-making process, in weapon aiming for example, and fine-tune his responses and the course of action he selects.

Where all this leads, inevitably, is to an old assumption that the pilot is becoming an expensive irrelevance, soon to be replaced by robotics and artificial intelligence. It would, so the argument runs, make more sense to put effort into super-sophisticated precision-guided missile technology and forget the 'weapons platform' and its pilot altogether. It is clear, however, that the manned aircraft can do things that missiles, however 'smart', cannot do. In looking at the conflicting plans for counterair war in Europe, for example, with each side attempting to win air superiority by attacking the other's airbases, it will be clear how close missile attack comes to theatre nuclear war and to the breakdown of the deterrent posture which conventional air power is there to uphold. Similarly, air power is highly flexible and can meet military needs very rapidly outside setpiece planning, as the Falklands fighting proved. Moreover, manned aircraft remain the only practical system for striking manoeuvring targets such as armour, mobile missile systems or dispersed, unprepared air bases.

The power of information technology may intrude upon the domain of the manned aircraft, as the section on the future of tactical air power and the 'air-land battle' concept may prove, but it looks as if the manned combat aircraft will be around for a long time to come.

West German Luftwaffe Tornados ready to scramble.

CHAPTER 1

Tactical Air Power

Air forces cannot occupy ground, seize cities or accept a surrender. They are essential adjuncts to the firepower and flexibility of land forces, which can do these things, and a vital shield for friendly land forces against enemy air power.

The first function, in historical terms, of air power is the gathering of intelligence about the adversary's intentions and dispositions. Today that reconnaissance mission involves satellites, very high-flying, special-purpose aircraft and remotely piloted vehicles, but the tactical reconnaissance aircraft, using high speed at low level for survival, is still an important combat type.

The second function is close air support which aims precise and flexible firepower against enemy troops and armour in contact with friendly forces. The third is interdiction, in which firepower is directed at the enemy's supply lines and his deep, logistic warfighting ability, and includes the destruction of enemy reserves or follow-on formations (sometimes called 'battlefield interdiction'). The fourth function is troop carrying and air resupply, which includes battlefield mobility using helicopters and paratroop operations.

The fifth function is to clear the sky of opposition in order to allow these other functions to be performed and, at the same time, to prevent the enemy from doing the same. This is the battle for air superiority and involves offensive and defensive, so-called counterair operations. The given mission may call for widely varying performance criteria. Aircraft used on interdiction missions do not necessarily require a highly manoeuvrable airframe, whereas an air-superiority fighter, for example, does. A close-support attack aircraft will not require the ability of a penetrating aircraft to fly very fast at low level.

For years, however, increasing costs and political pressure to rationalize meant that the old, dedicated single-mission types developed at the end of World War II were replaced, first by dual-capable strike/fighter jets and then by purpose-designed multi-role combat aircraft. These, it was hoped, could do everything from fleet air defence to deep-strike interdiction in northern European weather, all with a single basic airframe modified with appropriate avionics and weapons fit.

In the early 1970s a different concept was in the ascendant, certainly in the US, leading back to dedicated single-mission types. They were to form an air order of battle in what the USAF called a 'high-low' mix, combining expensive high-performance aircraft with simpler and cheaper counterparts.

Dedicated air-superiority aircraft themselves divide into such a sub-set of specialities. At one end are machines like the F-14 and F-15 which pack large radars and long-range missiles into a high-performance airframe and aim to make multi-target interceptions at beyond visual range. At the other end is the close-in dogfighter, surviving in combat through manoeuvrability and relying on gunfire and all-aspect, short-range missiles for offence.

The F-15 Eagle, with its great power and combat capability, was originally intended for air-to-air combat, with the lighter F-16 Fighting Falcons making the running in fair-weather fighting over the battlefield. The F-16 was developed by General Dynamics, paying close attention to what European NATO customers could afford. Ironically, at the outset of the 1980s, the F-15 and F-16 were both considered as bases for the USAF's derivative fighter programme, a machine loaded with sophisticated and expensive systems designed primarily for the air-to-ground mission. It seemed as if the multi-role combat aircraft had come full circle once again.

The original 'high-low' formula, with over 60% at the lower end of the mix, was based on the premise that any war in Europe would be savage and short, with aircraft destroyed at phenomenal rates. Thus, US planners at the time chose to rely on large numbers of relatively simple interceptors to win the battle for air superiority in air-to-air combat with the sheer mass of aircraft put up by Soviet Frontal Aviation, beating them with better technology and better weapons.

That comfortable assumption was overturned by the modernization of Frontal Aviation with highly capable air-superiority and interdiction aircraft, and the high-low concept was overturned with it. Final quantities of F-15 Eagles should amount to 1472. The later models of the planned total of 1388 F-16 Fighting Falcons are anything but austere and simple aircraft.

Counterair operations

Offensive counterair operations seek out and destroy competing air forces over disputed or hostile territory. This is by no means just a question of shooting enemy aircraft out of the sky in one-to-one combat. Enemy SAM sites, intercept radars and ground-control centres are the targets for the defence suppression mission using jamming aircraft and direct attack anti-radiation missiles, while AWACS aircraft would be priority targets for a counterair offensive.

Hostile air forces are most vulnerable when caught on the ground, a lesson taught over and over again in military history: the destruction of the Polish air force in 1939; the loss of 4000 aircraft, mostly on the ground, in the first week of the German invasion of the Soviet Union in July 1941; and the Six-Day War when Arab air forces were caught and destroyed at their bases in one day—June 5, 1967.

As two massively armed opponents confront each other in central Europe today—the air forces of the Warsaw Pact facing the air forces of NATO and the USAF Europe, each plans to win the counterair war in the classic manner, by attacking the other side's aircraft at their bases.

A pair of McDonnell Douglas F-15 Eagles of the USAF reveal their claws, Sparrow medium-range and Sidewinder short-range air-to-air missiles. Designed in the 1960s for service in the 1970s as an air superiority fighter, the F-15 is set for development into one of the most capable multi-mission aircraft in service with any air force.

Soviet offensive air operations are the key to any success on the ground, with the objective of denying NATO air superiority over the battlefield and over NATO rear areas. Frontal Aviation's air armies are 'echeloned', in the manner of Soviet ground forces, to thin out the targets for Nike Hercules nuclear area-defence surface-to-air missiles. In a counterair offensive these forces might be expected to attack in rapid successive waves, using conventional weapons in the first instance. The primary objective would be to destroy NATO's numerically inferior air forces before they could be reinforced from the continental United States. The first wave would suppress ground defences and the second would go for NATO's 25 main operating bases, with nuclear-capable aircraft as their primary targets. The third wave, comprising medium bombers, would go for deep counterair targets and secondary operating bases, fuel and logistic supplies, and nuclear weapon storage sites and launchers. Alternatively, medium- and short-

range missiles tipped with nuclear or chemical weapons might be the counterair weapon of first resort.

Without air superiority, it is realistic to assume that NATO has only three days before Soviet Frontal Aviation overwhelms its remaining air bases, when US reinforcement will no longer matter, let alone be possible. Of the 1400 NATO aircraft in place in the central region, about 500 are dedicated to air defence. In addition there are roughly 2000 non-nuclear SAM missiles on the western side and around 5000 anti-aircraft artillery pieces. These might face a penetrating hostile force of more than 1500 strike aircraft and 400 medium bombers.

NATO is hopeful of holding the line on the first day of any attack, but by the second day its 25 main air-bases would be crumbling, the sortie rate dropping rapidly and stocks of ready-use surface-to-air missiles running out. By the third day NATO might have lost control over its own territory, exposing its land forces

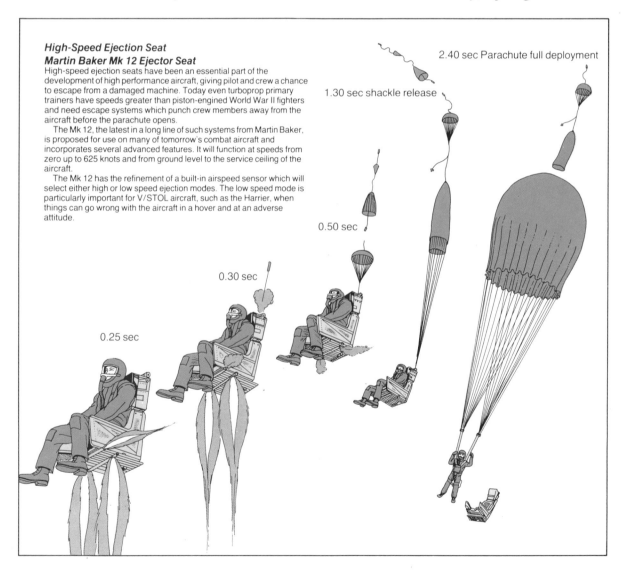

High-Speed Ejection Seat
Martin Baker Mk 12 Ejector Seat

High-speed ejection seats have been an essential part of the development of high performance aircraft, giving pilot and crew a chance to escape from a damaged machine. Today even turboprop primary trainers have speeds greater than piston-engined World War II fighters and need escape systems which punch crew members away from the aircraft before the parachute opens.

The Mk 12, the latest in a long line of such systems from Martin Baker, is proposed for use on many of tomorrow's combat aircraft and incorporates several advanced features. It will function at speeds from zero up to 625 knots and from ground level to the service ceiling of the aircraft.

The Mk 12 has the refinement of a built-in airspeed sensor which will select either high or low speed ejection modes. The low speed mode is particularly important for V/STOL aircraft, such as the Harrier, when things can go wrong with the aircraft in a hover and at an adverse attitude.

2.40 sec Parachute full deployment

1.30 sec shackle release

0.50 sec

0.30 sec

0.25 sec

to the lash of direct air attack by the surviving forces of Frontal Aviation.

This frightening timetable means that the only way of blunting Soviet air power would be to attack its bases with NATO's nuclear Quick Reaction Forces (QRA), available for SACEUR's Nuclear Operations Plan. These are currently dual-capable strike aircraft (F-111E/Fs), based in Great Britain, and Pershing Ia ballistic missiles, based in West Germany, to be supplemented or replaced by 1988 with 108 Pershing IIs and 562 ground-launched cruise missiles.

The current necessity of waging counterair warfare with *nuclear* weapons to have a chance of winning a *conventional* battle puts enormous pressure on those within NATO who advocate a shift to a doctrine of 'no first use' or even 'no early use' of nuclear weapons. They would point out the alternatives to nuclear-tipped missiles which, at present, are deep-strike ground-attack aircraft with all-weather capability, armed with special airfield attack weapons. They would further point out the promise of new-technology runway destructors and sub-munition dispensers mounted on super-accurate ballistic or cruise missiles which, some claim, could eliminate Warsaw Pact air power at a stroke.

Although modern airfields are heavily defended by SAMs and combat aircraft are dispersed in blast-proof shelters, they are still tied to thousands of metres of concrete—an F-15, for all its tremendous thrust, needs about 5000 ft of hard runway for typical combat operations. Thus, runways in particular have become the targets for a range of direct-attack and area-denial munitions to hinder their repair.

Interdiction

The counterair and interdiction missions are closely related. They both involve penetrating hostile airspace in all weathers and at night if necessary to attack targets, the destruction of which will produce a lessening of enemy combat power at the main point of contact. Soviet land forces are arranged in echelon formation, spread out to disperse the target that a

Above left: The Tornado, set to be the primary interdictor aircraft of several NATO air forces, designed to fly low on deep-strike penetration missions. *Above right:* The Su-24 Fencer, Soviet Frontal Aviation's equivalent of the Tornado, capable of flying strike missions deep into NATO's rear areas from East German bases.

mass army on the move might present to tactical nuclear weapons. The first echelon masses an immense concentration of firepower at the point of breakthrough but, if it burns out, the second or third echelon arrives to pierce the depleted defensive crust. Again, the defender's problem is the same as in counterair operations—to defeat a conventional attack by these so-called 'follow-on formations'. Moreover, the bridges, railheads and roads through which they draw their offensive strength must be constantly threatened, and, like the airfields, this too demands offensive operations very close to theatre nuclear warfare.

The capabilities of NATO's 500 or so all-weather penetrating aircraft, therefore, are of crucial importance in holding up the nuclear threshold in Europe. They have to penetrate a defensive screen of some 4000 counterair fighters, 6000 SAMs and 10,000 anti-aircraft artillery pieces. They have to generate a very large number of sorties (about 1000 a day) in order to hit the estimated 100 heavily defended key interdiction choke points, the 40 main operating base (MOB) airfields and the equal number of dispersed operating bases (DOBs) in East Germany, Poland and Czechoslovakia. They do not yet have the ability to destroy aircraft in hardened shelters with non-nuclear munitions.

Again, therefore, key interdiction and communication targets are components of NATO's Nuclear Operations Plan.

Whatever the utility of missiles for hitting fixed-site targets, the unique ability of manned aircraft is to attack mobile targets and dispersed air bases. The manned, penetrating strike aircraft is, therefore, very much part of contemporary air power and represents perhaps the most intensively engineered (and most expensive) class of tactical aircraft in service today.

The Tornado, although conceived as a multi-role combat aircraft, has emerged in its primary role as an interdictor strike-system designed to fly low and fast all the way to a target, and able to do so unerringly at night or in adverse weather, while carrying a very large load of conventional munitions. The RAF, meanwhile, has developed a dedicated long-range air-to-air variant with a different avionics and weapons fit.

The key to survival of an aircraft penetrating hostile defended territory is high speed at low level, made possible by terrain-following radar (TFR), which looks at the landscape ahead and below and generates computerized flight commands, and variable-geometry and advanced flight controls which smooth out the ride through the gusts and turbulence of low-level flight.

All front-line Soviet attack aircraft, from the Su-17 Fitter-C, by way of the MiG-27 Flogger F to the big airfield attack and interdiction specialist, the Su-24 Fencer, feature variable geometry in some degree. The Fencer was the first modern Soviet aircraft designed specifically for interdiction/strike and the first to carry a weapons officer in addition to the pilot, both sitting side by side as in the US F-111, which the Fencer closely resembles in layout if not in size. It caused almost as big a stir in the west as the appearance of the SS20 missile because of its advanced electronics and its large payload and range, which would allow it to reach the Irish Sea and return to bases in East Germany, or outflank NATO's forward air defences and come in from the rear.

Like Tornado, Fencer is designed for low-level

A West German Tornado is tended outside its hardened aircraft shelter. NATO airfields would be priority targets in the opening moves of a 'counterair' war.

penetration missions, with 50% of its all-up weight as fuel and warload, the same as comparable western types and a measure of its efficiency. It has terrain-following radar, an attack radar used in conjunction with a laser rangefinder, a weapon-management computer as well as Doppler navigation radar and autonomous INS, which allow large distances to be covered without ground reference. The pilot has an automatic flight-control system, a map display and a head-up display which projects aircraft management data and weapon sighting into his line of sight. Six external weapons stations can accommodate up to eight tons of bombs, and a 1000-kg nuclear bomb can be carried on the rear centre fuselage pylon. NATO expects at least 760 Fencers to be operational by 1987.

France's primary deep-strike interdiction aircraft of the late 1980s will be the Mirage 2000N, which flew for the first time in prototype form in 1983. It marks another return to the multi-mission type expressed in a single basic airframe. The two-seat Mirage 2000 reverts to the classic tailless delta formula of the Mirage III series of the 1950s. The aerodynamics are very advanced, and fly-by-wire computerized flight control allows a far-aft centre of gravity, improving manoeuvrability in combat and permitting a much-reduced landing speed. The low-wing loading of the delta layout, however, is totally unsuited to the attack role and the airframe is much more prone to bumps and gusts at low level than, for example, the Tornado. The 2000N has a crew of two, terrain-following radar, a very capable navigation system and advanced ECM equipment, and will be a platform for the nuclear-armed ASMP medium-range stand-off missile, operational from 1986.

However capable an individual aircraft may be, its

chances of successful penetration are in proportion to the capabilities of the air defences it is facing. Tornado, which took ten years to get into service from prototype, will have to trade off some of its offensive warload in order to keep up its penetration capabilities, carrying such self-defence weapons as Alarm anti-radiation missiles and Skyshadow ECM pods.

The tactical doctrine of most European NATO air forces favours fast, low-level ground attack missions by pairs of aircraft, with precision-guided munitions giving a high chance of successfully striking the target on the first pass. Current US doctrine for interdiction and close-support missions is somewhat different—it emphasizes stand-off attacks with smart weapons and is reluctant to make overflights of terminally defended targets (the United States pulled out of the development of the British JP233 airfield attack weapon because it involved overflying). Attacks would be made rather as a composite battlegroup operation—flown with air superiority cover and accompanied by defence-suppression and electronic warfare aircraft.

Some analysts in the United States are predicting that the next generation of strike aircraft may abandon low-level tactics altogether and with them all the difficulties of navigation, the strain on the airframe, extra fuel consumption, and the danger of bird strike and of being shot down by one's own side. The answer is operations at medium altitude, with Stealth and ECM contributing to survival and using supersonic cruise to dodge higher-altitude surface-to-air missiles. Indeed most Soviet SAMs are now optimized for low-level operation.

By the late 1980s the USAF's battlefield interdiction F-4 Phantoms will be on average 20 years old and the deep-strike F-111 fleet will be beginning to run down because of age. The F-15A and F-16A, although they have considerable secondary-attack capability, were not designed as long-ranging all-weather attack types.

The USAF has a long-term requirement for an F-15/F-16 replacement, called the advanced tactical fighter or ATF, but this would not even begin production until the mid-1990s. There are, meanwhile, two moves which can be made in the direction of the ATF: one is to modify the present F-15/F-16 fleet for air-to-ground roles without detracting from their air-to-air capabilities in a multi-stage improvement programme (MSIP); the second, the so-called 'derivative fighter programme', would take either of the existing aircraft yet to be delivered, but engineered from the outset as dual-capable types with emphasis on the air-to-ground mission.

The F-15 has already been manufactured in two major subtypes since its service debut in 1974 (the Bs and Ds are two-seat trainers). The F-15C has increased internal fuel and provision for conformal fuel tanks. F-15Cs of the 1st Tactical Fighter Wing, earmarked to support the Rapid Deployment Force, could for example, in theory self-deploy from Bitburg

The Tornado's variable-geometry wing allows it to fly in the all-important low level, under the radar sanctuary without shaking crew and airframe to bits.

in West Germany to the Persian Gulf using conformal tanks, a distance of 3200km.

Some 140 F-15A/Bs, earmarked for continental US air defence and ASAT duties, will not be retrofitted but 281 other As and Bs and 340 C/Ds will be re-engineered with new radar and avionics to operate AIM-7M Sparrow, AIM-9M Sidewinder and, eventually, AIM-120 AMRAAM, the advanced medium-range air-to-air missile which is a 'fire-and-forget' successor to Sparrow. Electronic counter countermeasures are being enhanced with a new radar warning receiver system, internal jammers, chaff and flare launchers, plus the jam-resistant Seek Talk HF voice communications and JTIDS digital information system.

Some 500 F-16 As and two-seat Bs serve in the USAF and roughly half that number again in other air forces. This aircraft, which began life as a lightweight fighter demonstrator, is being tested with an impressive array of the latest highly expensive systems, which give it medium-range air-to-air capability and formidable ground attack potential. Construction of the first-generation F-16As and two-seat Bs will tail off in 1984, when production of 662 F-16D F-16Cs and Ds will be under way. Under consideration for these aircraft are AMRAAM missiles and, for ground attack, the LANTIRN targeting and navigation pod, advanced Maverick air-to-ground missiles, Wasp anti-armour missiles, a low-altitude sub-munition

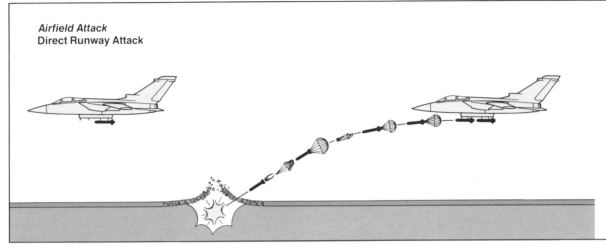

Airfield Attack
Direct Runway Attack

dispenser system and the General Electric 30-mm gun pod. Avionics and ECM updates will include Seek Talk, the Global Positioning System (GPS), the Airborne Self-Protection Jamming System (ASPJ), a new radar warning receiver and the Precision Location Strike System.

The derivative fighter

The second step towards the ATF is the derivative fighter programme which will take either the F-15 or F-16 in its final production batches and give their air-to-ground performance a significant boost as F-15Es or F-16Es. McDonnell-Douglas have been flying since 1980 a demonstrator called Strike Eagle with a specially equipped rear cockpit, laser designators, FLIR and synthetic aperture radar able to create electronically an image of ground targets. This aircraft, now referred to as the Advanced Fighter Capability Demonstrator (AFCD), is being tested, together with two other prototypes, against an F-16 derivative. This, unlike the F-15 AFCD which emphasizes new avionics in a barely altered airframe, concentrates on proving a radical new wing layout and a new engine. The F-16XL features a 'cranked arrow' wing and one demonstrator is flying with General Electric's F110 engine with digital control. The wing provides the best available balance between supersonic and subsonic lift/drag ratio and yet offers greater fuel capacity and less drag when loaded with underwing weapons than does the standard F-16 layout. Low-level penetration speed is quoted at Mach 0·9 and air-to-air performance is improved. In 1984 it was announced that the F-15E had been selected, with 392 aircraft due to begin delivery in 1988. The F-16XL will continue to be evaluated as a testbed for future F-16 developments.

The ATF programme

Beyond the F-15E is the USAF's advanced tactical fighter programme, a completely new combat aircraft, designed around emerging technology and planned to enter service at the beginning of the new century. The requirements for the ATF are exacting—it must better any Soviet opposition it is likely to

---

Dedicated anti-airfield weapons

DURANDAL Operational on French air force strike aircraft, Durandal is a powered bomb, launched at low level, parachute retrofitted, then accelerated very quickly to drill through concrete 40 cm thick and break up the runway by heaving effects. It is on order by the USAF.

BAP 100 A small, concrete-penetrating bomb carried in clusters of 18 by aircraft such as French air force Jaguars and in service with four other air forces. The launch sequence produces a wide spread of craters.

BRFA A Spanish-developed rocket-assisted runway penetration bomb; it has a damage radius of 180 m.

Soviet concrete 'dibbers' are known to be in use in both 250 and 500 kg sizes, the latter designated M62.

JP 233 A UK-developed anti-airfield weapon for low-level delivery by aircraft such as the Tornado, now entering production. The system consists of two distinct types of munition, 30 runway-cratering devices and 215 area-denial sub-munitions. Other sub-munition delivery systems under development include the French Pégase, the Franco-German Apache-CWS, the German NW-1 and the US Low Altitude Dispenser (LAD). This is configured as a winged canister which can be launched against targets from stand-off ranges of up to 20 km, using inertial or remote precision designation for guidance.

MRASM This is a development programme for an air-launch stand-off weapon for the US Navy and the US Air Force, based on the BGM-109 missile. The USAF version will carry anti-runway sub-munitions.

---

encounter in the 1990s and beyond, yet carry out air-superiority and deep-strike missions with ranges previously associated with specialized interdiction aircraft. ATF must be long-ranged, yet capable of operations from dispersed airstrips with a take-off length of 600 m. Stealth is less emphasized than STOL

Area Denial

Hardened aircraft shelter

because the demands on the airframe caused by high-speed operation and the integration of the weapons load are difficult to balance with stealth. However, the lowest possible radar cross-section and other observable factors are high priority. A reduction of two in radar cross-section, for example, may so degrade an intercept radar's performance that the aircraft will be inside the radar's *minimum* range within seconds of being picked up.

Seven US manufacturers under contract to the USAF are working on ATF proposals, with four apparent broad avenues of approach: a small, lightweight yet sophisticated aircraft affordable in large numbers; the 'supercruise' solution which applies advanced airframe concepts to extend the F-15's flight envelope, cruise and manoeuvrability into supersonic speeds; the 'YF-12' approach (a reference to the original interceptor-fighter version of the SR-71 Blackbird) to produce an aircraft capable of high-altitude, high supersonic cruise, dodging SAMs by speed and equipped with very powerful long-range radar and missiles; and, lastly, an approach emphasizing stealth and low visibility.

The ATF programme will be pushing at the boundaries of many technologies, including propulsion, digital avionics and crew survival, with ejector seats configured to operate with the aircraft at any angle, and high-altitude operation.

Air-to-air combat

In spite of the transformation of air-to-air combat conditions from an open cockpit at 100mph, with a synchronized .303 machine gun, to twice the speed of sound with radar-guided missiles, one rule of air warfare remains the same. Some 80% of air kills are the result of surprise, the victim not being even aware of his attacker until he was riddled with bullets or a missile blew him out of the sky. Therefore, the primary requirement of a combat aircraft and of pilot training is the ability to achieve surprise and to avoid being surprised in turn. For the 20% of cases where battle is actually joined, the third requirement will be the ability to outmanoeuvre and outshoot the opponent.

Aids to surprise in the attack are speed, electronic

Durandal runway attack weapons on test on a USAF F-111. The USAF has conducted extensive tests with alternative runway attack systems. Durandal requires direct attack by overflying the target at relatively low level.

silence and, coming out of the sun once in visual range, small size. Aids to detection are ground- and air-based surveillance radars, a jam-proof tactical communication system, on-board electronic counter-countermeasures and radar warning receivers, and good all-round pilot visibility. Fighters should patrol in pairs, each covering the other's blind spot.

No missile has yet been developed which will unerringly destroy its target, whatever evasive manoeuvres or countermeasures it employs. Once a dogfight has been joined, therefore, the way the weapons platform behaves will be as important as the abilities of the weapon system, and ther are no countermeasures against a stream of high-velocity shells from a rotary cannon firing 100 rounds a second.

Very high speed using afterburner consumes fuel and means that the fighter can do little else but fly in a straight line. At speeds above Mach 2, only attainable at high altitude, aircraft such as the Phantom, which are comparatively manoeuvrable at lower speeds, have a very large turn radius. What is more important is the rate of turn, measured in degrees per second, which is the unique capability of a particular airframe in its aerodynamics, power and structure to

The strike versions of the F-111 combine a heavy bombload with 'theatre' range, able to reach deep into Warsaw Pact territory from bases in eastern Britain.

'pull g', that is, to sustain the lateral acceleration forces of rapid manoeuvring.

In fact the pilot, not the machine, is the first limitation on sustainable g-force levels. At low altitude, where the wings can grip the thicker atmosphere for heavy rapid manoeuvring, a pilot can begin to black out at four g. The Eagle, on paper at least, can sustain nine g.

As a rule, the lower the wing loading, the greater the attainable rate of turn. However, this militates against the second priority for combat manoeuvrability, which is a high thrust-to-weight ratio and maximum acceleration. This demands a small, thin wing with minimum drag and high loading. Thus, the designer must find the most appropriate compromise between conflicting elements.

An important aspect of air combat is fuel management. As a rough guideline a fighter pilot can take his aircraft's total flying time and divide it into three periods: the first to reach the combat zone (the combat radius), the second for combat, and the third for returning to base. A typical fighter has a range of 2700 km and a cruising speed of 900 km, and thus a theoretical flying time of three hours. Supersonic speed, however, requires use of the afterburner which may triple the cruising speed but consumes the fuel at 20 times the normal rate. At full power an F-15 could consume its combat reserve fuel in less than three minutes. If there is not enough fuel left to reach a friendly base the aircraft will crash as surely as if it had been shot down. Therefore 'combat persistence' is another vital factor in aircraft design for air super-

iority. In a manoeuvring dogfight, the aircraft which breaks off first will be the most vulnerable. The aircraft which has the fuel to keep fighting or is still able to use the afterburner if necessary will have the advantage. This factor is sometimes called the fuel fraction—that is, the weight of internal fuel carried expressed as a percentage of the clean take-off weight, with guns loaded but no other external stores. Around 32% gives the maximum combat persistence. Less fuel is not enough, and above that level extra tankage leads to a falling off in overall performance.

Miniaturized digital computers, robotics and the first glimmers of artificial intelligence are set to reshape combat aircraft. The typical 'agile' layout, seen in various proposals for next-generation aircraft, such as the Israeli Lavi, the Swedish JA 39 Gripen and the FEFA 'Eurofighter', with canard forward wings and so-called control configured vehicle (CCV) layout, is made possible only by on-board computer power, which constantly reins in the aircraft's inherent instability by means of fly-by-wire controls. Computerized weapon aiming, meanwhile, cuts into the pilot's own decision making, refining his actions and editing inputs from the outside world to make his work load possible. Helmet sights and voice controls are set to transmit commands at almost the speed of thought.

Two such technologies have already been demonstrated on USAF-funded prototypes, which are certain to have enormous impact on the tactics and technology of air-to-air combat.

AFTI
The USAF's IFFC (integrated flight and fire control programme), called Firefly III, blends pilot and

Super Mirage 4000, clearly in the long line of Dassault deltas but as potent a combat aircraft for the '80s as its Soviet or US counterparts.

automatic commands in target tracking for both air-to-air and air-to-surface attacks. If the target is kept within a box projected on the pilot's head-up display, the system will take out any remaining errors. The most spectacular demonstration of the system's effectiveness was given in tests in Aug. 1982 when a modified F-15B shot down a rapidly manoeuvring PQM-102 target drone with gunfire from an unheard of 130° aspect, approaching from the front and from the side. The IFFC system was engaged at 3000-m range. Fire was opened at 1770 m and ceased two seconds later at 1160 m. In later tests bombs were dropped accurately during 3·5-g manoeuvres, the pilot following bank angle and g commands projected on the head-up display.

The AFTI (Advanced Fighter Technology Integration) F-16 demonstrator is designed to explore new airframe concepts and eventually combine them with an integrated flight and fire control system to produce an ultra-slippery, quick-reaction airframe. Critics might say that the same effect could be obtained by concentrating on smart weapon systems rather than the manned weapons platform itself.

The key to AFTI is on-board computer power which uses three powerful digital computers, 'voting' continuously to keep the inherently unstable airframe under constant control, a task beyond any human pilot, with perhaps 100 movements per second. There is an emergency analog system in each computer to get the pilot home, should all three digital systems fail.

Artificial stability

The use of vertical canard surfaces fitted to the intake of the AFTI demonstrator allows the aircraft's attitude to be 'decoupled' from its direction of flight. Its nose can be pointed left, right, up or down without the flight vector changing—rather like making a controlled skid in a car. Flat turns can be made without the aircraft rolling, and the aircraft can climb or descend without changing its angle of attack. Using the canards as 'snow ploughs' can lead to rapid deceleration in flight. Voice commands have been tested in the AFTI F-16, beginning in Dec. 1982. The 'vocabulary' of the Lear-Siegler developed system is 100 words and is linked to the multi-purpose displays, so that any push-button command can be made by voice. The pilot's hands are thus free to fly the aircraft and his eyes to scan for targets or threats. Because of voice commands, the manufacturers are proposing that a single-seater could in fact fulfil the very ambitious requirements of the USAF's advanced tactical fighter (ATF) programme.

European manufacturers, meanwhile, have shown themselves anxious to get into the agile combat aircraft business, both to meet the perceived defence needs of the 1990s and to keep domestic industries intact, and are reluctant to yield the high ground of technology entirely to the Americans. Acting alone they do not have the technical or production base to obtain a foothold but together they have a chance. The problem is that each air force has differing requirements and replacement needs. An agile air-to-air capability is less important when contemplating the need to replace ground-attack aircraft for example.

The RAF drew up Air Staff Target 396 in 1969,

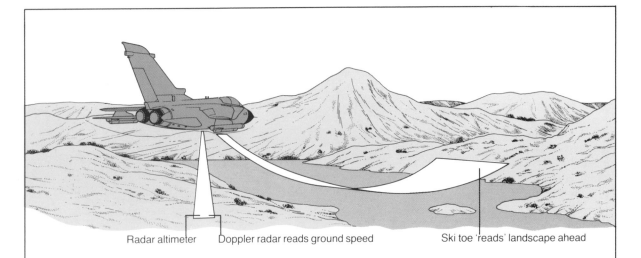

Radar altimeter   Doppler radar reads ground speed   Ski toe 'reads' landscape ahead

Terrain-following Radar

An interdictor strike aircraft, like the Tornado G.R.3, is one of the most complex and sophisticated of modern weapon systems. The only way to get through the nets of surface-to-air missiles and hostile acquisition radars is to fly in the sanctuary beneath enemy radar coverage.

To fly at low level at high speed and in bad weather demands highly sophisticated aerodynamics and onboard avionics to make the human task feasible. The Tornado's variable geometry airframe, for example, smooths out the bumps and turbulence of low-level flight which would shake the crew of a conventional fixed-wing aircraft to pieces.

Similarly, the Tornado pilot has a terrain-following radar to enable him to fly so fast, so close to the ground. A forward-looking electronic 'ski toe' reads the landscape ahead of the aircraft and feeds instructions into the flight computer. A radar altimeter gives an accurate precise height reading while down-looking Doppler radar provides an exact measurement of speed over the ground.

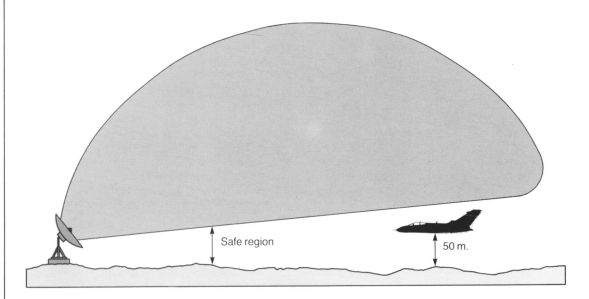

Safe region   50 m.

Flying under the Radar

The need for penetrating aircraft to fly low is dictated by the capabilities of hostile air defence surveillance radars which have a blind spot below the horizon as radar beams cannot follow the curvature of the earth.

This blind spot is taken up several degrees above the horizon because of interference between the main beam and the surface of the earth, creating a 'safe' region of approximately 50 metres. However, atmospheric conditions can cause distortion in the beam's coverage and regions of anomalous propagation where the radar will not function properly.

The natural safe region can be extended by resort to jamming and the use of active EW measures such as missiles which home on the source of radar emissions. The USAF operates such specialist aircraft as the F-4G Wild Weasel and EF-111A anti-radiation and airborne jamming platforms, while MBB is developing an electronic combat and reconnaissance variant of the Tornado for the German Navy and the RAF may follow.

calling for an all-weather, ultra-STOL-capable aircraft eventually to replace the Harrier and Jaguar in the strike role. STOL was removed on the grounds of expense, but by now the project was so like Tornado that it was not worth continuing. A new requirement, AST 403, called for a simple Harrier/Jaguar replacement without the all-weather capability.

In 1979 the RAF issued AST 409 for a Harrier replacement which was filled by the AV-8B (Harrier GR 5). Meanwhile, the request for a 'manoeuvrable Jaguar', to be in service by 1987, was still in mid-air. Looking round for European partners, the British found that the French wanted a Jaguar replacement later and that the Germans needed a super-agile air-superiority aircraft to replace their Phantoms, rather than a ground-attack type with secondary air-to-air capability.

Although this European Combat Aircraft (ECA) proposal did not last long, a Eurofighter has finally emerged with 'agility' as its key capability. In Dec. 1983 five air forces issued a joint air staff target for a Future European Fighter Aircraft (FEFA), a programme that could result in 800 aircraft, 200 each for Britain, France and West Germany, and 100 each for Italy and Spain, with an in-service date of 1995.

The industrial partners in the original ECA programme, BAe, Dassault Bréguet of France and MBB of West Germany, broadly agreed on its layout—a single-seat, twin-engine delta canard with artificial stability. When the programme broke down the manufacturers continued to work independently on agile designs. BAe produced the P110, which became the so-called agile combat aircraft (ACA) when the Panavia partners, MBB and Aeritalia, joined in at an industrial level. Meanwhile, the British Ministry of Defence is providing funding to build a flying technology demonstrator, although this is not a service prototype. This contract was announced on the eve of the Paris air show where Dassault Bréguet revealed its rival ACX, again showing the now familiar canard-delta layout and advanced digital avionics. Both prototypes are due to fly in 1986. So far West Germany has refused to commit itself to joining either programme, while an Anglo-French industrial clash of interest has intensified the rivalry. Tornado production will be phased out in 1989, leaving BAe without a combat aircraft programme. Dassault, meanwhile, has only just begun production of the Mirage 2000 which, until a European agile fighter is produced, will be the only non-US contender on the export market.

Export fighters

The classic formula used by relatively small national manufacturers to extend their production runs is to secure export orders, but there is a large gap between the cost of highly capital-intensive aircraft designed for use in a European war and what Third World or newly industrialized clients may be able to afford. The outstanding export successes of recent times have

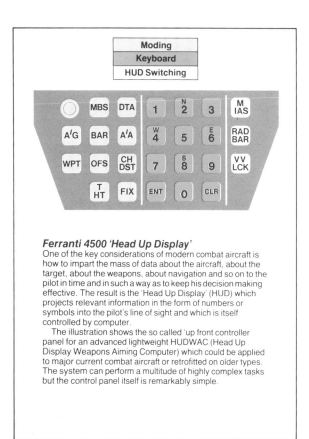

Ferranti 4500 'Head Up Display'
One of the key considerations of modern combat aircraft is how to impart the mass of data about the aircraft, about the target, about the weapons, about navigation and so on to the pilot in time and in such a way as to keep his decision making effective. The result is the 'Head Up Display' (HUD) which projects relevant information in the form of numbers or symbols into the pilot's line of sight and which is itself controlled by computer.

The illustration shows the so called 'up front controller' panel for an advanced lightweight HUDWAC (Head Up Display Weapons Aiming Computer) which could be applied to major current combat aircraft or retrofitted on older types. The system can perform a multitude of highly complex tasks but the control panel itself is remarkably simple.

been the French Dassault Mirage III and the US Northrop F-5, designed from the outset as low-cost export fighters and often directly funded by US military assistance programmes. Dassault has flown a Mirage III Nouvelle Génération, which incorporates fixed canard surfaces, a new, more powerful airframe, plus fly-by-wire controls and the nav-attack system derived from the Mirage 2000. The result is a vastly more capable aircraft. Similarly, the Northrop F-20 Tigershark has taken the F-5 format and built in the latest avionics to produce a quick-reaction fighter with great combat power. The company has to be confident of selling 300 + aircraft before launching production and is keeping a close eye on developments affecting the rival Mirage IIING and the changing needs of Middle East customers. Israel's Kfir, a developed version of the original Mirage III, is another export hopeful.

However slippery its airframe and however well provided with avionics and warning devices, an aircraft will survive in combat only if its weapons are up to the mark. An air-to-air missile presents the same design challenges as does a combat aircraft itself, only on a smaller scale. The missile has to fly through the air under continuous power, with a motor configured to deliver the appropriate speed to overhaul supersonic aircraft and the appropriate range before it burns out. It has to be able to outmanoeuvre its target, while guiding itself on to it through electronic and physical countermeasures, and disregard natural distractions.

The choice of guidance principle largely depends on the expected operational range. All air-to-air missile guidance depends on the principle of a seeking head acquiring energy from the target aircraft and generating commands by means of on-board electronics, to steer itself by movements of its control services or by vectoring nozzles towards the source of that energy.

An infrared-seeking missile homes in on the heat emitted by the target's jet efflux or produced by the effect of friction on its airframe. The most effective infrared-guided missile will have 'all-aspect' capability, that is, it will home in on a hot target from any angle and not simply be restricted to a tail chase. Moreover, it will disregard such distractions as the sun, the ground or IRCM flares. Heat-seeking missiles generally operate at ranges below 10 km, the exception being the infrared-guided version of the Soviet AA-6 Acrid AAM, which operates in tandem with radar-guided missiles at ranges up to 20 km.

Semi-active homers

The current generation of medium-range missile, with ranges up to 30 km, operate by 'semi-active homing': they home on radar energy originated by the large radar of the launch aircraft reflected by the target. The technique requires continuous illumination of the target by the attacker, which is no handicap in a chase from behind but is a grave disadvantage in a head-on closing engagement.

The third method is to give the missile its own onboard active guidance, with enough power to transmit its own energy and home on the received reflections. The latest model, AIM-54C Phoenix AAM, arming F-14 fleet defence fighters, flies on inertial guidance in the general direction of the target and to a point in the sky predicted by computer. When in range, its own radar becomes live. Earlier models use semi-active homing in the cruise phase, the F-14's very capable AWG-9 radar providing the initial illumination at ranges up to 200 km.

Since the advent of radar, flying low has been a way of evading ground-based surveillance radars and of confounding air-launched missile radars by hiding in the 'clutter' of ground reflections. The perfection of pulse Doppler radar in the 1960s gave so-called 'lookdown shoot-down' capability to airborne radars. The computer sorts out echoes that are apparently retreating in the same direction and at the same velocity as the aircraft—that means they are stationary on the ground. Anything moving in a dissimilar pattern below will show up therefore as a Moving Target Indication (MTI).

Dissimilar air combat

In spite of the advent of radar-guided air-to-air missiles capable of operating far beyond visual range, many air combat fighters have simple radars purely for target acquisition and gunsight ranging at ranges down to 8 km. Pitching such a machine against the big, dedicated air-superiority aircraft with semi-active homers having a 70-km range might seem a pointless exercise, but if the rules of engagement require visual identification first, then the game suddenly comes live. In Vietnam, for example, US pilots had to identify targets visually to avoid shooting down Chinese aircraft and found that their air-to-air missiles, originally designed to destroy bombers with straight and level shots from astern, could not be launched in tight turns against rapidly manoeuvring, lightweight North Vietnamese MiGs.

Air Intercept Missile Evaluation (AIMVAL) tests conducted in 1977 at Tactical Air Command's vast weapon test facility at Nellis AFB, Nevada, pitted F-14 Tomcats and air force F-15s armed with Sparrow semi-active homers against F-5Es of the so-called aggressor force's squadrons, trained to simulate potential enemy aircraft in Dissimilar Air Combat Training (DACT). The F-5s were armed with AIM-9M all-angle-capable Sidewinders and the rules demanded visual identification, so that the Sparrow's ten-to-one range advantage was wiped out. The F-14s picked up the bogey F-5s at 16 km using TVSUs (TV Sighting Units) and duly fired their missiles (using electronic simulation), but had to remain on intercept course to provide continuous radar illumination. The F-5s would launch a 'fire-and-forget' Sidewinder as soon as they picked up the big aircraft. The F-5s went down a few seconds later, but so did the Tomcats and the F-15s, caught up in the mass aerial destruction which left very few theoretical survivors.

Simultaneously ACEVAL (Air Combat Evaluation) studies, conducted to see how different force levels affected the battle, found that the more aircraft involved, the more the technological advantages of the F-14s and F-15s were eroded.

In one-to-one combat the Eagle had a three-to-one advantage. As soon as numbers went beyond four,

Left: The USAF's F-16 AFTI (Advanced Fighter Technology Integrator) can make 'instantaneous' flight manoeuvres unlike any other aircraft. *Right:* A Sea Harrier pilot takes on a Mirage in a simulator. Like AFTI, such techniques are made possible by computer power.

Air Combat Manoeuvres

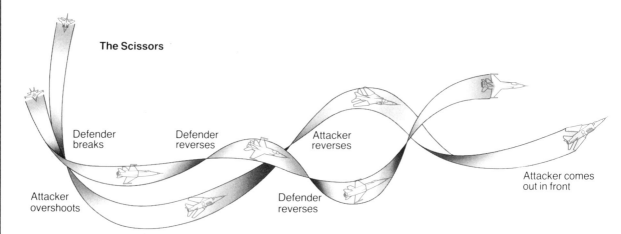

The Scissors

Defender
breaks

Defender
reverses

Attacker
reverses

Attacker comes
out in front

Attacker
overshoots

Defender
reverses

The Scissors

Seen from the point of view of the defender this manoeuvre is designed to turn the tables on a pursuer and force him out in front. The initial turn of the Scissors is reversed when it is clear the attacker has in fact overshot and is wide of the defender's vulnerable rear before reversing as shown.

The Scissors are performed under full power throughout but with the nose trimmed up to reduce forward speed – airbrakes can also be used for sudden deceleration but they tend to give away the defender's intentions. The essence of the Scissors is reducing the forward velocity vector, the straight line along which the twists and turns are made. The fighter which effects this most efficiently will emerge on the tail of his opponent and thus in the ideal position for attack.

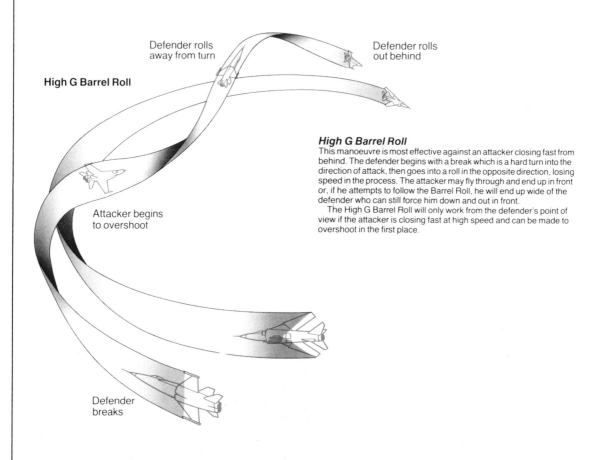

Defender rolls
away from turn

Defender rolls
out behind

High G Barrel Roll

Attacker begins
to overshoot

High G Barrel Roll

This manoeuvre is most effective against an attacker closing fast from behind. The defender begins with a break which is a hard turn into the direction of attack, then goes into a roll in the opposite direction, losing speed in the process. The attacker may fly through and end up in front or, if he attempts to follow the Barrel Roll, he will end up wide of the defender who can still force him down and out in front.

The High G Barrel Roll will only work from the defender's point of view if the attacker is closing fast at high speed and can be made to overshoot in the first place.

Defender
breaks

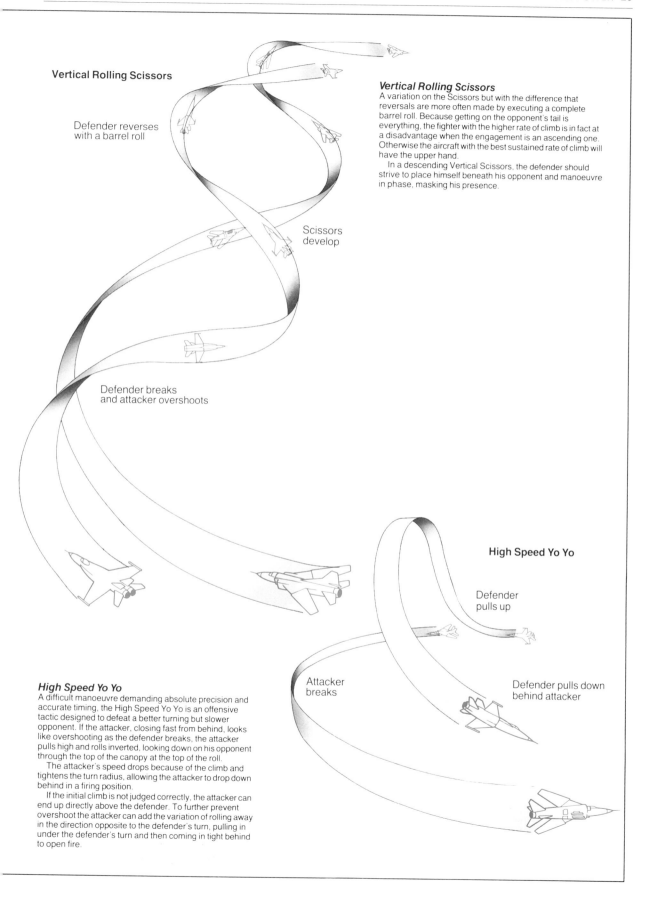

Vertical Rolling Scissors

Defender reverses
with a barrel roll

Scissors
develop

Defender breaks
and attacker overshoots

Vertical Rolling Scissors

A variation on the Scissors but with the difference that
reversals are more often made by executing a complete
barrel roll. Because getting on the opponent's tail is
everything, the fighter with the higher rate of climb is in fact at
a disadvantage when the engagement is an ascending one.
Otherwise the aircraft with the best sustained rate of climb will
have the upper hand.

In a descending Vertical Scissors, the defender should
strive to place himself beneath his opponent and manoeuvre
in phase, masking his presence.

High Speed Yo Yo

Defender
pulls up

Attacker
breaks

Defender pulls down
behind attacker

High Speed Yo Yo

A difficult manoeuvre demanding absolute precision and
accurate timing, the High Speed Yo Yo is an offensive
tactic designed to defeat a better turning but slower
opponent. If the attacker, closing fast from behind, looks
like overshooting as the defender breaks, the attacker
pulls high and rolls inverted, looking down on his opponent
through the top of the canopy at the top of the roll.

The attacker's speed drops because of the climb and
tightens the turn radius, allowing the attacker to drop down
behind in a firing position.

If the initial climb is not judged correctly, the attacker can
end up directly above the defender. To further prevent
overshoot the attacker can add the variation of rolling away
in the direction opposite to the defender's turn, pulling in
under the defender's turn and then coming in tight behind
to open fire.

This British Aerospace 'agile' combat aircraft proposal dates from the early 1980s when the project was looking for funds.

communications became overloaded and skilled F-5 pilots devised lock-breaking manoeuvres (such as flying at 90° to the flight line of the pursuer to negate the pulse Doppler look-down radar capability) in order to defeat the big radars hunting for them and, once dogfighting began, the Eagle's kill-ratio dropped dramatically.

Today, TAC pilots receive far more intensive training in dissimilar air combat than they did in the late 1970s, both at Nellis in the very large-scale 'Red Flag' exercises at on-base ranges, and in advanced computer-generated cockpit combat simulators. Meanwhile electro-optical enhanced-vision devices have improved and the latest Northrop TCS, equipping a proportion of the US Navy's F-14s, can give visual identification of combat aircraft at more than 30 km and distinguish a Boeing 707 at 70 km in clear skies. The lessons of simulated air combat underline the need both for a successor to the semi-active-homing missile and for a true, medium-range 'fire-and-forget' system. The planned successor to Sparrow is AMRAAM, the advanced, medium-range air-to-air missile which is a joint NATO programme to produce a weapon compatible with the F-14, F-15, F-16, F-18, Tornado, and other NATO air-defence and air-superiority aircraft of the late 1980s and the 1990s.

An AMRAAM engagement begins when the launch aircraft radar acquires and tracks the target. The weapon control system supplies the missile's own on-board computer with the co-ordinates of a point in the sky where it is predicted that the target will be. The missile is launched and flies on inertial guidance to that point where the active seeker switches on and the missile completes the intercept. The missile is electronically silent in its mid-course phase and theoretically immune to countermeasures. Thus the launch aircraft can either monitor its progress or break away. The missile flies at Mach 4 to overhaul targets which might be escaping at Mach 2 and has an advanced proximity fuse to ensure the maximum destructive effects.

The complement to AMRAAM, which is being built in the United States, is ASRAAM, the advanced short-range air-to-air missile, which will provide the successor to Sidewinder and is being developed by an Anglo-German consortium.

Guns

Air-to-air missiles are very expensive ($70,000 for a Sidewinder, double that for a Sparrow) and, once they are all fired, the combat aircraft is defenceless. The six-barrel Vulcan M61 rotary cannon, developed in the mid-1950s, is the standard US aircraft gun armament. Technology programmes using liquid propellant or caseless ammunition have so far failed to provide an effective replacement. The exceptional GAU-8/A fires 30-mm armour-piercing projectiles at very high muzzle velocities and is specifically tailored to the needs of the tank-killing A-10 ground-attack aircraft. Most Soviet combat aircraft have at least one large-calibre internal gun and attack types carry additional podded guns under the wings or on the fuselage centreline.

Ground attack and close air support

The complex technology of counterair warfare, from runway destructors to long-range, air-to-air missiles, is all geared to clear the sky of hostile aircraft so as to enable air power to get to grips with the land battle.

Soviet Frontal Aviation is a specialist in air-to-ground warfare and is operationally structured to act in support of the primary land-based service. Most of the 16 Soviet military districts have a tactical air army attached and four more are assigned to the group of forces in Eastern Europe. In time of war, they would all come under the control of a front-level combined arms commander, flying and fighting very much as part of the Soviet combined-arms concept. While there has always been heavy emphasis on defensive counterair, Frontal Aviation would seek to apply offensive shock power on a large scale.

Most new Soviet aircraft in production are designed for deep-strike and ground-attack missions, with a far

The USAF practises extensive dissimilar air combat training, grouping aircraft such as this F-5 in special 'Aggressor' squadrons.

greater payload and range than their predecessors. In the 1960s the MiG-17, -19 and -21 were Frontal Aviation's front-line air-superiority fighters, with the Sukhoi Su-7 giving some ground attack potential. Poor all-weather and range/payload capabilities put offensive counterair and interdiction effectively out of reach, while electronic countermeasures were feeble. All that has changed—new aircraft such as the MiG-23, MiG-27 and Su-24 have delivered far better air-superiority, ground-attack and interdiction capability. In addition, the Soviet Union has put great effort into getting large numbers of ground-based electronic warfare systems into the field in support of the air battle, although these may not yet match US or Western European technical sophistication.

Just as significant is the development of 'smart' air-to-surface munitions, such as laser-guided anti-armour bombs and laser-homing, helicopter-launched antitank missiles. Meanwhile, the newest types to appear in the Frontal Aviation line-up include dedicated anti-armour types very much in the US A-10 and attack helicopter mould—the Su-25 Frogfoot and the Mi-24 Hind-E. The latter has been described as a 'low-speed, ground-attack fighter' rather than an attack helicopter.

Close air support is one of the most difficult and contentious of combat missions. The difficulties of distinguishing friend from foe have been lessened somewhat by the advent of precision guidance, but the deterrent effect of ground-based air defence degrades accuracies. Pilots who practise close air-support missions admit that the best method currently available of hitting a target without overflying is to toss a cluster bomb at it. The need to fly low and fast to achieve surprise and give air defence the minimum target has led to the development of a wide range of area weapons to compensate for the aiming errors inherent in such attacks. Unguided rockets launched in barrages remain effective ways of attacking infantry and armour and such an attack, from an Argentine Navy light trainer, sank the Royal Navy frigate HMS *Ardent* in Falkland Sound.

Vastly improved ground-based air defence also prohibits the old technique of close air support (CAS), whereby aircraft would orbit the battlefield looking for targets, waiting for guidance from ground-based forward air controllers (FAC). These are now too limited in their area coverage and too easily lost.

The sheer tonnage of conventional munitions needed to destroy dispersed armour is another problem. West German studies showed that to destroy a Soviet breakthrough group—consisting of 500 tanks, 500 armoured vehicles, 50 artillery batteries, 200 SAMs, and 300 trucks—approximately 5500 sorties were required in order to deliver some 33,000 tons of gravity bombs. Separate US Department of Defense studies showed that an aircraft that attacks a tank formation with cluster bombs under combat conditions has only a 50% chance of destroying a single tank in the first pass.

The Dassault Mirage III Nouvelle Génération is a strong contender for export to expanding Third World air forces.

Specialized attack aircraft

The USAF developed a requirement for a dedicated close air-support aircraft in its Attack Experimental (A-X) programme of 1967. A competitive fly-off between two prototypes, the Northrop A-9 and Fairchild Republic's A-10, resulted in the A-10's selection and the first operational squadron was formed in 1977. Production of aircraft was completed in 1983.

The A-10A Thunderbolt II is very unlike any other warplane. It is designed to fly low and slowly, to absorb shell hits if necessary and survive, and yet deliver a formidable weight of munitions. It mounts the enormous GAU-8/A 30-mm rotary cannon in the nose, firing armour-piercing shells with depleted uranium penetrators, and with a rate of fire sufficient to destroy any known armour.

Its capacity to survive air and ground threats is built up from its low working altitude (at which interceptors cannot operate), its manoeuvrability, its ground defence suppression and countermeasures, its extensive armour protection for the pilot and critical systems, an airframe designed to absorb damage, plus co-operative flying techniques with other A-10s and attack helicopters.

A typical sortie might begin at a secondary operating base, which could be a strip of Autobahn. Armed with 1000 rounds for the 30-mm cannon, and either four TV-guided Mavericks (*see* below) or, in adverse weather, six Rockeye cluster bombs or Snakeye retarded bombs, the A-10s should be available for close air support at five minutes' notice, with four aircraft on station in each US Corps area on NATO's centre sector during daylight hours.

A new doctrine, called Joint Air Attack Team, has been evolved for the maximum effectiveness of A-10 operations. Under this system, on a typical mission the A-10s are briefed, then despatched to a forward air-holding area. Next an airborne forward-air controller assigns them to a target area where a ground FAC in a Light Observation Helicopter (LOH) allots an array of targets.

Army AH-IQ Cobra helicopters will be on the scene

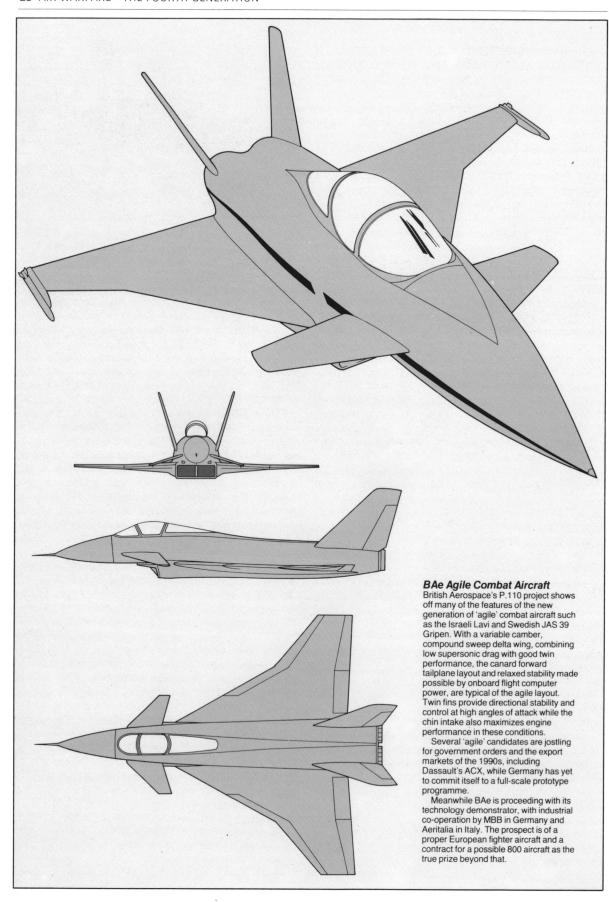

BAe Agile Combat Aircraft

British Aerospace's P.110 project shows off many of the features of the new generation of 'agile' combat aircraft such as the Israeli Lavi and Swedish JAS 39 Gripen. With a variable camber, compound sweep delta wing, combining low supersonic drag with good twin performance, the canard forward tailplane layout and relaxed stability made possible by onboard flight computer power, are typical of the agile layout. Twin fins provide directional stability and control at high angles of attack while the chin intake also maximizes engine performance in these conditions.

Several 'agile' candidates are jostling for government orders and the export markets of the 1990s, including Dassault's ACX, while Germany has yet to commit itself to a full-scale prototype programme.

Meanwhile BAe is proceeding with its technology demonstrator, with industrial co-operation by MBB in Germany and Aeritalia in Italy. The prospect is of a proper European fighter aircraft and a contract for a possible 800 aircraft as the true prize beyond that.

by this time, engaging the priority ground air defence targets such as ZSU-2 3-4 multiple cannon with TOW missiles and calling up artillery support where necessary.

Briefed by the FAC in his rapidly manoeuvring light observation helicopter, the A-10s enter the target area flying at around 50 ft and using terrain for cover where possible. The A-10s will operate in loose pairs, going into attack separately. At a distance of two miles the first aircraft will rise up momentarily to acquire a target, then open fire with the cannon at 4000 ft slant range, breaking away at 3000 ft to avoid the air defences. The second aircraft stands off at between 4000 and 12,000 ft, ready to engage any air-defence weapon with a Maverick TV-guided air-to-surface missile while selecting a target for gun attack. Meanwhile, the first A-10 is lining up to protect the second aircraft's rear.

The A-10 (now joined in its unique class by the Soviet Frogfoot, which has been operational in Afghanistan) represents an extremely specialized weapons platform adapted for a distinct role. Much more typical are strike aircraft such as the RAF Harrier GR.3 and the Anglo-French Jaguar, which would make fast, low passes over enemy armour using cluster or laser-guided bombs. The Harrier GR.3 is unique in NATO's inventory in being able to

The Israeli Lavi new-generation combat aircraft displays the by now familiar 'agile' features including canard foreplanes.

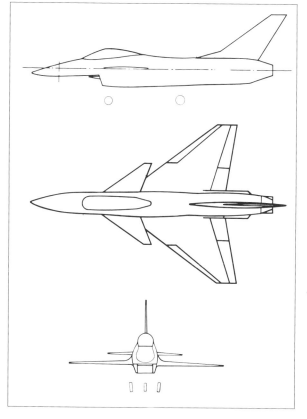

Top: The Israeli Kfir-C7 dual-role interceptor and ground attack aircraft, based on an extensively redesigned Mirage 5, is a contender in the export market. *Above:* The Northrop F-20 Tigershark which traces its lineage back to the F-5 Freedom Fighter has been expressly designed for export.

operate from roughly prepared, dispersed sites and its V/STOL capability frees it from dependence on all-too vulnerable concrete runways, although not from logistic support. At present this support relies on wheeled vehicles, but will progressively shift to Chinook helicopters. In the Falklands fighting Harrier GR.3s, which had been wired to operate Sidewinders in the air defence role, were rapidly converted back for ground-attack operations once the Sea Harriers had proved their effectiveness in establishing air superiority. Around 150 missions were flown by the GR.3s, at first from ships at sea, then, in the final advance, from grass strips. Apparently, CAS sorties were flown using map grid references for targeting, but in the final hours before the surrender a series of highly successful sorties were made, using Paveway bombs, against targets marked by ground-operated laser designators.

The light-attack aircraft is one of the most numerous in world air force inventories, partly because it is far smaller and simpler in its systems and avionics than the super-sophisticated penetrators designed for a NATO war. The A-4 Skyhawk, originally designed in the early 1950s as a US carrier-based attack aircraft, has proved itself time and time again in Israeli hands. Flown by Argentine pilots, it might have been far more effective against the British task force in the Falklands if it had been equipped with correctly fused iron bombs or more sophisticated air-to-surface weapons.

The West German Luftwaffe has replaced the G.91 in the ground-attack role with the Alpha Jet two-seat strike trainer which, in spite of its small size, can still lift 2500 kg of precision-guided munitions. Beginning in 1987, the Italian air force will replace its G.91s

with the equally diminutive AM-X, jointly developed by Aeritalia and EMBRAER of Brazil to provide a low-cost, subsonic, multirole combat aircraft, optimized for manoeuvrability at low level rather than high speed.

Air-to-surface weapons

An aircraft in flight presents a distinct target against a background of sky to the homing head of a guided missile. Targets on the ground, however, can be made indistinguishable from their surroundings by simple camouflage, even before the fog of battle or the murk of north European weather closes over them.

The first problem, therefore, is target acquisition and, although reconnaissance and forward air control may provide the exact co-ordinates of a target array, the necessarily high closing speeds at low level mean that the old methods of waypoint and stop-watch are no longer enough. Similarly, if the enemy chooses to attack at night or in bad weather he will enjoy instant air superiority if the close air-support force cannot fly or find him. The second problem is target designation—high-speed attack at low level is not the ideal way to deliver bombs precisely on an enemy who is in contact with friendly troops.

Close air support, therefore, increasingly shows the

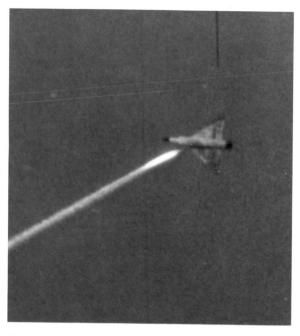

Left: An F-15C Eagle shows off its missile load and the FAST packs (fuel and sensor, tactical), fitting flush along the fuselage sides, which greatly extend range and sensor options.

Above: An AIM-9L Sidewinder achieves a head-on kill on a target drone. Such 'all-aspect' capability has had a great impact on the tactics and technology of air-to-air combat.
Below: AIM-7E Sparrows mounted semi-flush beneath the fuselage of a USAF F-4C with AIM-9P Sidewinders on the wing rack. The Sparrows rely on the launch aircraft's radar for continuous guidance.

Missile Homing Techniques

Heat-Seeking

The simplest form of air-to-air missile (AAM) is the heat seeker, homing on the heat source of a target aircraft representing and interpreting its infrared emissions via its guidance electronics into steering controls. Early models only worked in a stern chase, homing on a hot jet exhaust pipe but the new generation are 'all-aspect', that is, able to attack from any angle, and are able to distinguish much more accurately a real target from distractions such as the sun or the earth's surface. They need cryogenic cooling of their seeker head and can still be confounded by infrared (IR) countermeasures such as flares.

Semi-active homing

Heat seekers only function at relatively short range. Current medium-range AAMs are of the semi-active radar homing (SARH) variety which rely on the powerful radar of the launch aircraft to first find, then continue to 'illuminate' the target. The missile's much smaller radar seeker receives the powerful returns coming from the target and homes on them, using its own radar actively, only in the terminal phase. Semi-active radar launch platforms, however, must continue to illuminate the target throughout the engagement and thus are themselves vulnerable to shorter-range missiles in return.

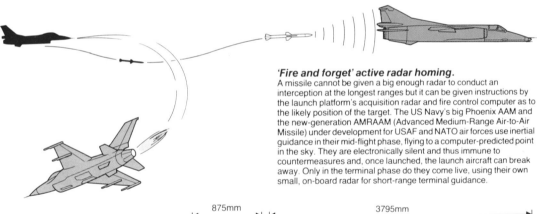

'Fire and forget' active radar homing.

A missile cannot be given a big enough radar to conduct an interception at the longest ranges but it can be given instructions by the launch platform's acquisition radar and fire control computer as to the likely position of the target. The US Navy's big Phoenix AAM and the new-generation AMRAAM (Advanced Medium-Range Air-to-Air Missile) under development for USAF and NATO air forces use inertial guidance in their mid-flight phase, flying to a computer-predicted point in the sky. They are electronically silent and thus immune to countermeasures and, once launched, the launch aircraft can break away. Only in the terminal phase do they come live, using their own small, on-board radar for short-range terminal guidance.

Matra Super 530

An air-to-air missile presents its designers with problems akin to that of the aircraft that launches it. It must have the right aerodynamics and range for the job it is intended to do, and the maximum electronic 'smartness'. The Super 530 can make intercepts at high speed and at high altitude with its long, thin wings and has a very high acceleration motor. It uses semi-active homing for guidance.

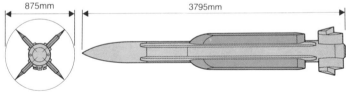

875mm   3795mm

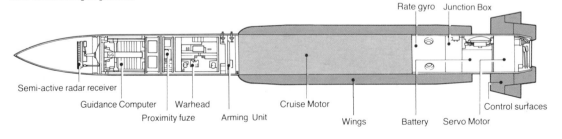

Rate gyro   Junction Box

Semi-active radar receiver
Guidance Computer
Proximity fuze
Warhead
Arming Unit
Cruise Motor
Wings
Battery
Servo Motor
Control surfaces

Air-to-air missiles

France

MATRA R530 All-weather all-aspect air-to-air missile (AAM) with range up to 18 km. Alternative semi-active radar homing (SARH) or infrared guidance (IR). In service with French and 12 other air forces. Developed version called Super 530 has twice the range and very fast acceleration.

MATRA R550 MAGIC AAM designed for close combat (launch from less than 5·5 to 6 km). Can withstand very fast manoeuvring with twist-and-steer control effected by forward canard fins. It arms a wide range of aircraft in service with 16 air forces including Mirage series, Super Etendard and Indian Navy Sea Harriers. Under development is a medium-range 'fire-and-forget' missile to succeed the Super 530 series codenamed MICA.

International

AMRAAM (AIM-120A) Advanced medium-range AAM to supplant AIM-7 Sparrow series, to be compatible with US and NATO air defence and air superiority aircraft of 1980s and 1990s.

ASRAAM A complement to AMRAAM and being developed by a European consortium, ASRAAM is planned to be the successor to Sidewinder by the 1990s.

Israel

PYTHON 3 Advanced infrared homing AAM with a range between 0·5 and 15 km. Apparently operational in air battles over Lebanon in mid-1982.

SHAFRIR Simple but effective short-range AAM with infrared guidance. Some 200 kills were credited to Shafrir during the Oct. 1973 conflict.

Japan

MITSUBISHI AAM-1 Sidewinder type infrared-guided AAM. Being replaced by AAM-2 which has high dogfight capability.

South Africa

KUKRI Dogfight missile with infrared guidance, with target aquisition supplied by pilot's helmet sight.

Soviet Union

AA-4 ACRID Large long-range AAM forming standard armament of MiG-25 Foxbat interceptor and Su-15 interceptor. Thought to be launched in pairs, each with inertial mid-course guidance and successively active and infrared-seeking terminal guidance.

AA-5 ASH Large long-range AAM associated with Tu Fiddler long-range interceptor.

AA-7 APEX Medium-range AAM comparable to SU Sparrow. Both radar-guided and infrared-homing models have been reported, a pair of each forming the standard armament of MiG-23 Flogger B fighters.

AA-8 APHID Small, close-combat AAM with infra-red and radar guidance reported on MiG-23 Flogger, MiG-21 Fishbed and naval Yak-36 Forger. The AA-8 is thought to be a replacement for the original AA-2 Atoll—equivalent to the early model Sidewinder, which also serves widely with the air forces of Soviet client states.

United Kingdom

SKY FLASH British development of US Raytheon Sparrow with SARH guidance. Skyflash is designed for all-aspect attack and to be able to intercept high- or low-speed targets at high or low altitude, with a snap-up and snap-down capability, picking out targets from ground clutter or ECM if necessary. Range is up to 40 km. The missile arms RAF Phantoms and will arm Tornado F2s. Built under licence in Sweden, Skyflash also arms the JA 37 Viggen in the interceptor role.

USA

PHOENIX AIM-54A Very capable and very expensive long-range AAM for fleet air defence, arming the F-14 Tomcat. Has mid-course inertial guidance and its own active radar terminal guidance. Improved AIM-54C model in small-scale production has digital avionics and enhanced ECM resistance.

SIDEWINDER AIM-9 SERIES The original Sidewinder dates back to the 1950s and the early days of infrared technology. The principle worked but the resulting missile was only really effective in tail chases against non-manoeuvring bomber targets. The essence of the missile was cheapness and simplicity and this has been retained throughout a long development and manufacturing cycle, while the capability of the seeker has been vastly extended. Large numbers of the early model, AIM-9J, entered production in 1970. The J model introduced double-delta canard control surfaces, giving it a much better dogfight capability. Sidewinder B, E and Js, early models in the US inventory, are being upgraded to the latest AIM-9P standard. The third-generation Sidewinder is the AIM-9L and M, which introduced a coolant bottle in the seeker head, permitting greater target resolution and all-aspect capability, the missile homing on to any friction-heated part of the target airframe and not just the jet exhaust. The latest M model has electronic improvements for screening out infrared countermeasures and a smokeless motor.

SPARROW The present AIM-7F is the fourth generation of this important medium-range AAM, arming USAF and USN interceptor aircraft. Sparrow functions by semi-active radar homing with a range of up to 60 km, and miniaturization of the guidance electronics has left room for a bigger motor, increasing the range to 100 km. A new model AIM-7 is being developed with greater ECM resistance and improved look-down, shoot-down capability.

application of two results of emerging technology—forward-looking infrared (FLIR) and laser target designation—while dual-purpose fighters will have a multi-mode radar, able to function in air-to-air combat or to provide navigation and attack functions.

A FLIR system works very much like a TV camera, but instead of visible light it uses heat to resolve a picture. It can display a picture of the landscape ahead built up from contours of heat (scrub, rock vegetation and so on), together with any man or machines moving upon it. FLIR systems can be pod-mounted on existing strike aircraft and are being engineered from new into the 1980s generation of attack aircraft and helicopters.

The dual-purpose, air-to-air and air-to-ground F-16 has the Westinghouse AN/APG-66 radar, which will track air targets above or below the horizon, but is also equipped with eight separate air-to-surface modes for navigation and surface strike. There are three mapping modes which 'read' the landscape ahead, providing the pilot with an all-weather moving map display. In one mode the map can be frozen and the passage of the aircraft indicated by a computer-generated cursor taking inputs from the F-16's inertial navigation system. This means that, once in the target area, the aircraft can navigate without making radar emissions.

The air-to-ground ranging mode measures the distance to a designated target, supplying information to the fire control computer for accurate weapon release. There are two sea-surface attack modes for detection of ship targets in various sea states. The Sea 2 mode, which is used to screen out wave clutter, can also detect moving targets on the ground.

By adding the so-called 'synthetic aperture' method, the limited ability of airborne radar to distinguish static ground targets can be greatly enhanced. It uses the Doppler technique to distinguish closely spaced ground targets, the necessary Doppler shift being provided by the aircraft's own relative motion. A computer sorts out the signals and electronically synthesizes a picture of the landscape and any target array. The Hughes AN/APG-63 is the standard multi-mode radar of the F-15 Eagle. Modified to incorporate synthetic aperture techniques, the radar has been tested in the company-sponsored F-15 'Strike Eagle' attack fighter demonstrator and is claimed to have a resolution ten times better than previous airborne tactical radar maps.

When the aircraft has successfully navigated to the scene of action and picked out the target with the aid of FLIR or air-ground radar, the refinement of laser designation can be added to actually turn a ground target into an active if unwilling emitter of signals on which weapons can home.

Laser-guided bombs (LGBs) were first successfully tested at the US Armament Development and Test Center at Eglin AFB in 1966. Thus began the Paveway project, in which Texas Instruments developed add-on guidance kits for the USAF's standard high-explosive bomb. In this system a

Above right: The A-10A Thunderbolt II, the USAF's purpose-designed tank killer. The nosewheel and gun are offset, so the firing barrel of the 30-mm GAU-8/A Avenger cannon is always on the centreline.
Below right: The Avenger is designed to do this to tanks.
Below: The GE M197 triple-barrel 20-mm aircraft cannon has been turret-mounted in helicopters or in pods for fixed-wing strike aircraft.

Laser Designation

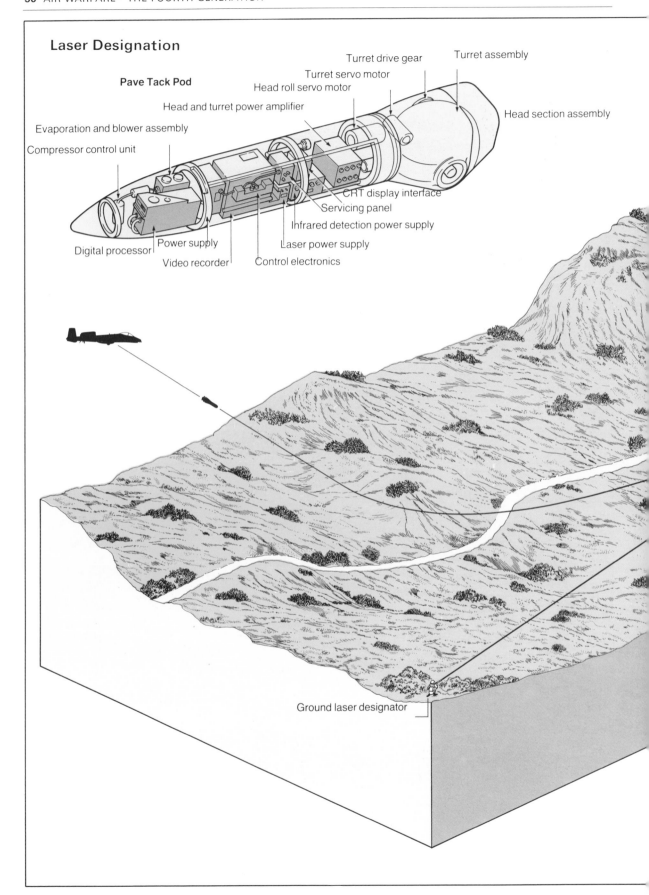

Pave Tack Pod

Turret drive gear
Turret servo motor
Head roll servo motor
Turret assembly
Head and turret power amplifier
Head section assembly
Evaporation and blower assembly
Compressor control unit
CRT display interface
Servicing panel
Infrared detection power supply
Digital processor
Power supply
Laser power supply
Video recorder
Control electronics

Ground laser designator

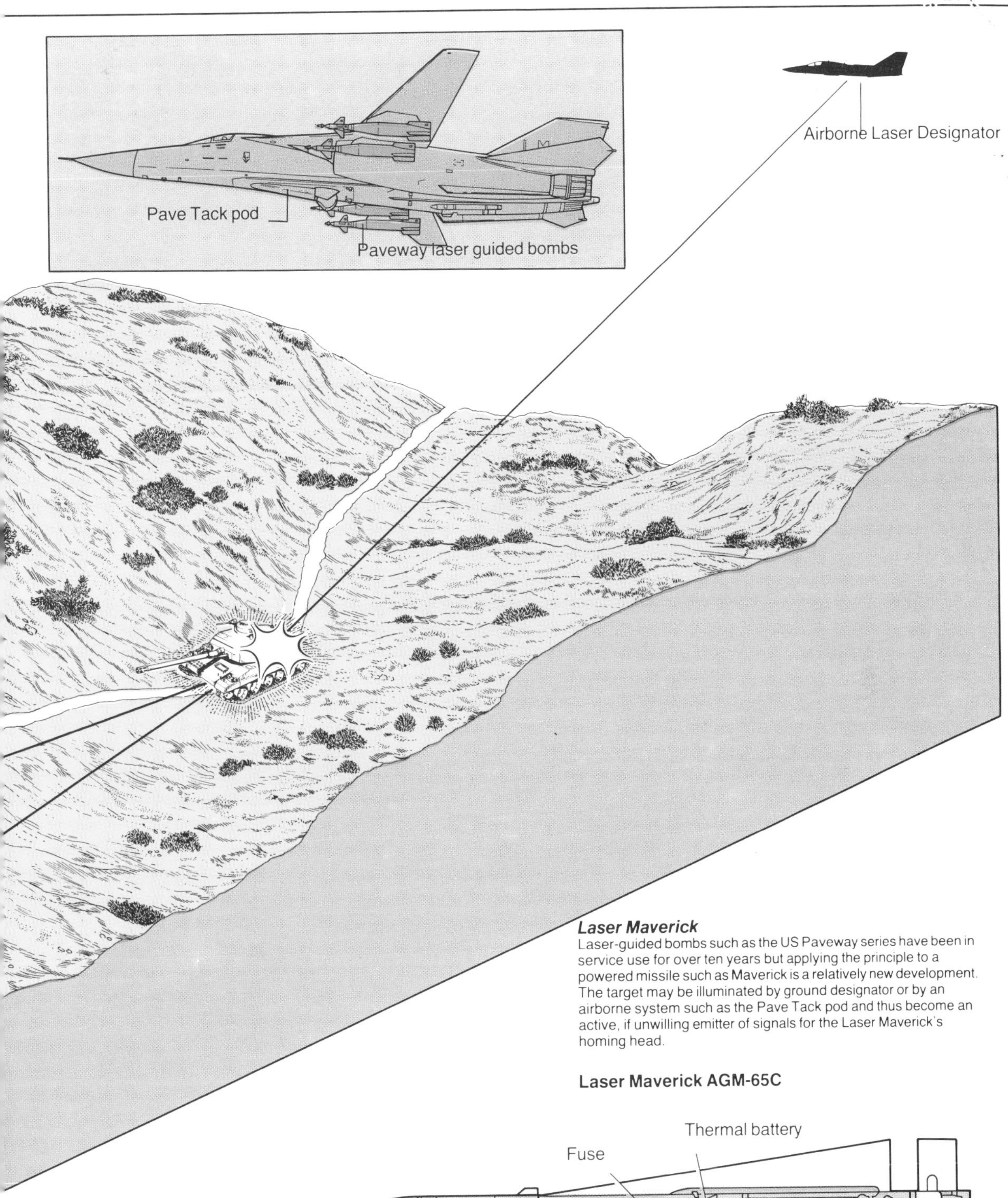

Airborne Laser Designator

Pave Tack pod

Paveway laser guided bombs

Laser Maverick

Laser-guided bombs such as the US Paveway series have been in service use for over ten years but applying the principle to a powered missile such as Maverick is a relatively new development. The target may be illuminated by ground designator or by an airborne system such as the Pave Tack pod and thus become an active, if unwilling emitter of signals for the Laser Maverick's homing head.

Laser Maverick AGM-65C

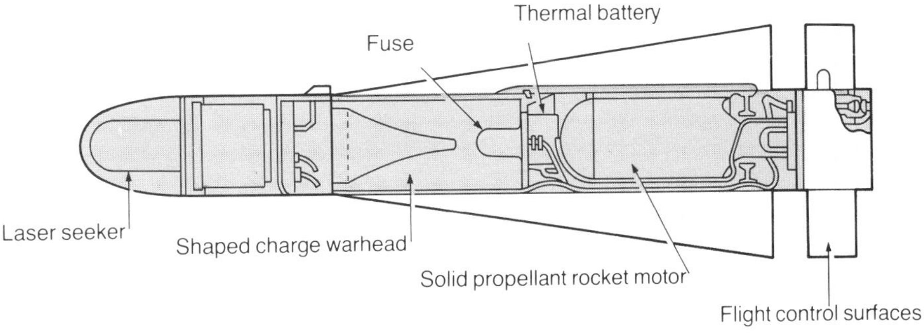

Thermal battery

Fuse

Laser seeker

Shaped charge warhead

Solid propellant rocket motor

Flight control surfaces

Above: A pair of A-10As show off their underwing stores to good effect—Mavericks and Westinghouse ALQ-119 electronic countermeasures pods. Both aircraft have Pave Penny laser seekers mounted just ahead of the cockpit below the fuselage. Target designation is effected by forward air controllers, either in helicopters or on the ground. The Pave Penny system is designed to track such 'sparkled' targets and provide weapons-aiming information through to the pilot's head-up display. *Below left and right:* Microseconds before and then (*the moment of*) impact upon a target tank by an AGM-65 Maverick.

pencil-thin beam of light laser energy is directed at the target from a remote designator, which may be operated by infantry on the ground or shot from a drone, an aircraft or a helicopter.

The target is now illuminated, reflecting scattered energy pulsed in a pre-set code in all directions. If a laser-guided weapon is now launched, its seeker will filter out all but the infrared transmissions, reading the pulses for the correct code. If it all adds up, the seeker head will steer itself towards the source of energy, taking the missile or the free-fall bomb with it.

The RAF uses US Paveway bombs (having abandoned development of its own LGBs) as do the air forces of Australia, Greece, the Netherlands, Saudi Arabia, South Korea, Taiwan and Thailand. The French began an LGB programme in 1978 and had it operational and ready for export in 1983. The Soviet Union, meanwhile, was in 1981 reported to be introducing a 500-kg LGB.

Laser designation also applies to powered air-to-surface missiles, such as the French AS.30 Laser and the US Laser Maverick. The Maverick is a very important ASM (more than 28,000 have been manufactured), with a shaped charge of high explosive for blasting through armour or reinforced concrete. The initial model was television-guided—it has a TV camera in its nose generating a picture which the pilot could read on his own screen. Once the tracker was slewed on to a target and locked on, the missile's own computer would guide the missile

on to it. For operations involving close support of friendly ground forces a laser homing version and an imaging infrared version able to operate at night or in adverse weather have been developed.

In contrast to weapons designed to arrive on target with pinpoint precision, other air-to-surface munitions are designed to spread their destructive power over a wide area. Some fire as a weapon in napalm bombs or mix fuel and air in an aerosol cloud before detonation. Alternatively, they divide their destructive power into smaller packages of sub-munitions.

Weapon design tailors munitions to perform specific attack roles according to the type of target—by blast, by fire, by enhanced blast with a longer pulse of over-pressure, by fragmentation, armour piercing, anti-personnel, earth penetration, concrete demolition, runway destruction, time-delay area denial and so on. Several of these characteristics can be combined in cluster bombs or strewn about from specialized sub-munition dispensers. The US CBU-24 cluster bomb contains 655 Sadeye sub-munitions, each one of which has a filler of high explosive in which 600 steel shards are embedded, lethal up to a range of 40 ft. Combining three types of fuse will produce a mixture of air burst, ground burst and delayed action, which will detonate after troops have come out of protective cover. The effects of a simultaneous CBU attack have been described as the equivalent of a well-aimed mortar barrage with six hundred 8-mm rounds landing at once.

Laser designators

Ground-attack aircraft carry laser designators and/or laser-marked target seekers. Jaguars and Harriers, for example, have a laser seeker in the nose which picks up pulsed laser energy from a target marked by a ground designator at ranges beyond pilot vision. The seeker interprets this as weapon-aiming information for the pilot, who may then launch Paveway-type bombs with their own autonomous laser homing heads. Pave Penny is the equivalent system on USAF A-7s, A-10s and F-16s. The US Pave Spike, in contrast, is an airborne designator with a gimballed beam-pointing system which can illuminate a target from a manoeuvring aircraft at stand-off ranges. Pave Spike is standard equipment on USAF F-4s and RAF Buccaneers in the strike role.

There are reservations about the actual operational efficiency of the current generation of designators. Carriers of airborne designators must orbit dangerously high, while the attacker drops his bombs and runs. The ground designator is vulnerable to detection and reliant on jam-free communications with the attacking aircraft.

The US Pave Tack system combines laser designation and range finding with other electro-optical systems which allow the acquisition and designation of targets at night or in adverse weather. The system uses a laser and a forward-looking infrared (FLIR) unit in a stabilized turret, which can be slewed and held on to a target during a wide spectrum of evasive aircraft manoeuvres. Pointing the pod forward provides a night-vision terrain avoidance system. Planned technology improvements include automatic target tracking, relieving the operator of having

Precision-guided munitions

There is little distinction between powered air-to-surface missiles and 'smart' bombs and glide bombs which rely on kinetic energy to reach the target once released. Guidance systems include wire- and radio-command guidance, laser homing and various optical applications such as TV and imaging infrared.

France
LASER-GUIDED BOMBS Matra and Thomson—CSF have developed a series of LGB kits for application on 250-, 400- and 1000-kg bombs and use in conjunction with ATLIS II laser designator. Bombs can be launched at low level at high subsonic speeds, allowing stand-off ranges up to 10 km, with several degrees of lateral offset from the target.
AS 30 LASER The successor to the command-guided AS 30 ASM, it is a homing, supersonic stand-off missile used in conjunction with ATLIS II designator or ground-based systems.

Soviet Union
AS-X-10 The provisional NATO designation for the reported Mach 0·8, laser-guided ASM arming MiG-27, Su-17 and Su-19 strike aircraft.
AS-X-1i The reported Soviet equivalent of US Maverick, using electro-optical guidance with a possible range of up to 40 km. Laser-guided bombs are also reported to be under development.

United States
BULLPUP AGM-12 A command-guidance weapon deployed on US aircraft from the late 1950s but no longer in service. Built by a European consortium, it still arms European NATO strike aircraft. Mach 2 speed over 17 km range.

WALLEYE I AND II Primarily a US Navy weapon, Walleye is a smart bomb born out of the experience of the Vietnam War, and has a TV camera in the nose. The TV and its guidance logic are locked on to a target and autonomously home upon it, allowing the launch aircraft to take evasive action. Walleye II is larger, with extended range and a data link to allow target acquisition and lock-on after launch.
MAVERICK Numerically the most important USAF air-to-surface missile, it possesses a range of guidance techniques, with either an anti-hard target or a blast fragmentation warhead. Initially developed with TV guidance functioning in the same manner as Walleye—19,000 AGM-65As are in the USAF inventory, together with 7000 AGM-65Bs with scene magnification allowing longer-range identification of small targets. AGM-65C uses laser guidance. After extensive tests it has been judged effective in the close support role if the target is illuminated by a stabilized ground- or aircraft-mounted designator. Hand-held designators are apparently effective only against large or static targets. The imaging infrared Maverick (AGM-65D) has been recently introduced and can function like TV Maverick, but in darkness or smoke or against camouflaged targets.
GBU-15 MODULAR GLIDE BOMB Conversion system for standard bombs to stand-off guided weapons by fitting electro-optical or imaging infrared TV seeker, data link to aircraft and planar or cruciform wings for glide. Aircraft being converted to carry these weapons are F-4E, B-52D, F-111F, F-15 and F-16.

The original development of laser-guided bombs began with the Paveway series in 1966, followed by Paveway II in the mid-1970s. The add-on housing heads are compatible with the Mk 82 500 lb, Mk 83 1000 lb and Mk 84 2000 lb GP bombs, and British Mk 13/18 1000 lb. Development of Paveway III series began in 1980-1 to provide free-fall weapons which can be delivered from very low altitude, yet at long stand-off ranges.

Above: The French Matra company have developed laser-guided bomb kits as add-ons for standard French air force bombs. This Mirage F.1 mounts an LGB plus a Matra 550 Magic AAM on the outer wing pylon. The Matra weapon has a flight time of up to 30 seconds.

Below: An AS 30 laser-guided, powered missile impacts on a laser designated test stand after launch from a Jaguar aircraft. The missile flight is in two phases, mid flight relying on gyro reference and terminal homing via the Thomson-CSF Ariel homing head.

The primary close support aircraft of Royal Air Force Germany is the Harrier GR 3. These aircraft are armed with underwing, unguided SNEB rocket pods plus two 30-mm Aden gun pods under the fuselage.

to keep the target in his monitor. Some 180 F-111s are being converted to carry Pave Tack.

LANTIRN (Low Altitude Navigation, Targeting Infra-Red Night) is the name of a controversial (by nature of its expense) programme to develop a podded navigation and laser-based target designation system that will give single-seat aircraft, such as the A-10 and F-16, an all-weather, precision-strike capability.

Air strike beyond the manned aircraft

The contradictions involved in mounting sophisticated smart munitions which could as well be missile-delivered on equally sophisticated and expensive manned weapons platforms have been recognized and eagerly exploited by rival services hungry for research funds. The US Army's Air-Land Battle concept paper, published in 1982, envisaged land war in the year 2000 as an ultra fast-moving fluid affair, with blended air-land forces battling from laser-armed hovercraft, with RPVs and missiles dominating the battle for airspace.

The USAF's *Air Force 2000*, published in Oct. 1982, sees the air battle as the traditional one, if not fought along traditional lines. The battle for air superiority is joined by a battle for superiority in space, while long-range manned systems, such as the ATF, will be necessary to interdict enemy land and naval forces, and have the flexibility to provide close air support.

Both services have been edged into co-operation on new weapon systems which, in fact, reflect rather the US Army's view of things—depending on missile delivery of smart munitions rather than manned penetrating aircraft. They are the JTACMS (Joint Tactical Missile System) suitable for air- or ground-launch, although led in development by US Army Missile Command, and the related JSTARS programme (Joint Surveillance Target Attack Radar System) which will provide the target information and will be an airborne system led by the USAF.

JTACMS will be a range of closely related missiles, including a Lance replacement for the Army, and an

---

Cluster bombs and area weapons

France

GIBOULÉE Bomblet dispenser system arming Mirage IIIs and Jaguars, designed for low-altitude attacks on tanks with armour-piercing sub-munitions or for carrying fragmentation bomblets to be used in attacks on infantry or trucks.

BELOUGA Free-fall bomb which is parachute-braked after release from high-speed, low-level aircraft. During descent it releases anti-armour, fragmentation or area-denial grenades, which are also individually braked and reach the ground vertically in a homogeneous pattern.

West Germany

MW-I MEHRZWECKWAFFE Multi-purpose container carried beneath Tornado, enabling attacks on airfields or armour concentrations at high speed and at low level. Can carry anti-armour sub-munitions, mines, anti-runway devices or hardened hangar penetrators.

Israel

RAL CLUSTER BOMB Anti-armour free-fall bomb containing 279 500 gm bomblets which disperse when the casing splits open in flight.

South Africa

MK II ALPHA Anti-personnel fragmentation weapon used with SAAF Canberra light bombers, strewn from containers with 25 bomblets each.

Sweden

VIRGO 120-kg fragmentation bomb arming A35 Draken and AJ37 Viggen aircraft in strike role.

Soviet Union

Cluster bombs have been in service on FA attack aircraft for a number of years and are adapted for incendiary, fragmentation and anti-armour attack.

United Kingdom

BL775 Primary anti-armour weapon of RAF attack aircraft including Harrier GR.3, Buccaneer and Harrier. BL775 is pre-set before take-off, with one of four time-delays between aircraft release and the bomb splitting open to dispense 147 bomblets in a timed pattern. Also used by several other air forces.

United States

ROCKEYE Operational since 1968, the Rockeye Mk 20 is in service with the USAF, the US Navy and the Israeli air force. Designed for attacks against heavy armour with 247 bomblets. A supplemental weapon has been developed with 717 anti-personnel and anti-truck sub-munitions.

CBU-SERIES More than 50 separate types of cluster bomb units (CBUs) have been developed in dispensing bomblets adapted for anti-personnel fragmentation, for use as incendiaries, as containers for nerve gas, incapacitant gas, or delayed-action napalm, or for use as mines.

FUEL-AIR MUNITIONS Fuel-Air Explosives (FAE) work by creating an aerosol of liquid explosive detonated in the air to produce very high overpressure (up to 300 psi has been reported) on the ground and have long been a development avenue for mine-clearing operations. Types in service include CBU-55 and CBU-72 cluster bombs, BLU-76/B with propane filling and others which are used with helicopters.

air-launch version to be carried on aircraft ranging in size from the F-16 to the B-52 bomber. However they might be launched, JTACMS would be guided into action by the JSTARS radar into a 'basket' above the target area, where they would dispense their smart sub-munitions. These, using infrared or millimetre-wave miniaturized radar seekers, would be able to 'recognize' a tank outline and home on to individual armoured targets, attacking the top plating where the armour is, in fact, thinnest. The sub-munition-dispensing mechanism can select area attack or line attack, along the length of a road convoy, for example.

Steering this hugely ambitious and expensive programme to completion in the face of political, funding and interservice rivalry problems will not be easy and, meanwhile, the USAF's derivative fighter is still being designed around the old Mk 82 iron bomb. However, it is hoped that the building-in of planned product improvements, like the F-15 and F-16 multi-stage improvement plan, will give the programme a chance. JTACMS could be operational by 1988, first with simple inertial guidance and accurate enough to hit fixed targets such as airfields. Meanwhile the system could be integrated with PLSS, a system already operational on high-flying TR-1s, able to look deep into hostile territory from stand-off range and fix precisely the positions of enemy radars.

After PLSS might come integration with GPS, the satellite-based global positioning system, and JSTARS itself, which would at last give missiles the ability to make a precision strike against moving targets—the last domain, perhaps, of the manned aircraft.

The Army intends mounting JSTARS on OV-1D Mohawk battlefield surveillance aircraft. The USAF has to decide whether the combination of sensors and control platform aboard a C-18 (Boeing 707) makes more sense than mounting sensors on a high-flying TR-1, with ground-based control and relay.

Above: Flight tests of the West German MW-1 (Mehrzweckwaffe—multi-purpose weapon) on the Tornado. A container beneath the fuselage can strew a variety of sub-munitions over a wide area. *Below:* The HB 875 area-denial sub-munition component of the British JP 233 low-altitude airfield attack system. Thirty runway-cratering devices are carried per system, along with 215 HB 876 delayed-action mines to hinder repair operations.

The Lockheed RT TR-1 is an update of the U-2 'spyplane', carrying powerful sideways-looking radar, able to 'see' deep beyond NATO's borders. The TR-1 is a possible candidate for carrying advanced target acquisition and designation systems which could transform the face of land warfare and tactical air operations.

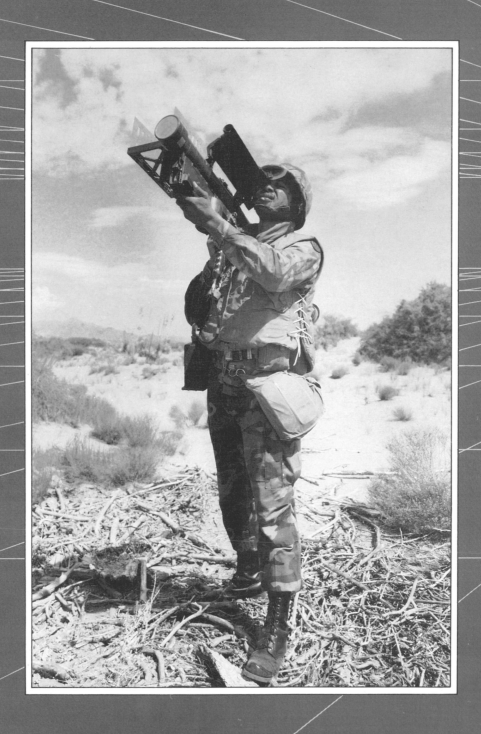

CHAPTER 2

Air Defence

Most sovereign states have deployed a system of national air defence based on a 'ground environment' of radar stations and a secure communication net, which are often integrated with civilian air traffic control (ATC). The actual forces available for the protection of national airspace, however, can vary from a handful of aging fighters to dense belts of surface-to-air missiles (SAMs) and thousands of dedicated interceptor aircraft. In areas of maximum military concentration such as NATO's Central Sector or the Middle East, the concerns of tactical and strategic air defence overlap almost completely to form a constant component of so-called counterair operations.

Offensive counterair operations aim to seek out and destroy competing air forces in hostile territory—attacking missile sites, blinding radars, and generally jamming and dislocating communications while shooting the enemy out of the sky in air-to-air combat. But enemy aircraft are most vulnerable when caught on the ground. Although the aircraft themselves are likely to be dispersed in hardened shelters, they are still dependent on thousands of metres of concrete runway, which are now the target for a variety of specialized airfield attack weapons (*see* chapter on tactical air power). Defensive counterair efforts strive to identify, track and designate intruders, then intercept them in the air or shoot them down from the ground.

The goal of counterair operations is to achieve air superiority, a degree of dominance over disputed airspace which will prevent the enemy from interfering prohibitively with one's own operations. But, even if general air superiority is achieved, the opponent may be able to attain local or temporary air superiority and one friendly sector may be denied air cover in order to achieve air superiority somewhere else. For these reasons air forces and ground forces have had to develop the doctrines and the technical systems for interlocking air-to-air operations with ground-based air defence, of which perhaps the greatest problem is the correct identification of friend and foe (IFF).

This chapter is concerned, therefore, with two distinct aspects of air defence—fixed defences based on long-range radars, emplaced missiles and assigned anti-bomber interceptor aircraft with specific peacetime duties of enforcing airspace sovereignty, and the tactically mobile systems employed by armies in the field.

As land warfare comes ever more to resemble war at sea, with men moving and fighting on land from within machines, so land-based air defence comes to resemble ever more closely shipborne missile defence. The same imperatives apply: an army formation, like a naval task force, must at all times be covered by an umbrella of air defence with interlocking long-range, short-range and last-ditch systems. Target and threat information must be acquired and processed by electronic means at the earliest possible opportunity

and a suitable response always be ready. Identification of friend or foe and target priorities must be established by computer in a matter of microseconds and a response made which will get through the attacker's electronic countermeasures. In an age of 'smart' bombs and precision-guided air-to-surface munitions, with the area destructive power near to that of a low-yield nuclear weapon, ground-based air defence takes on a tremendous urgency and its technology begins to overlap more and more with that of the combat aircraft it is facing.

Land-based air defence does not simply act by destroying enemy aircraft and wearing down the numbers, but also by deflecting or degrading the accuracy of the attack. If precision-guided munitions and electronics greatly multiply the attacking power of conventionally armed aircraft, the very need to engage equally sophisticated ground defence and load up with special-purpose weapons such as anti-radar missiles will divert them from their true effective purpose—aiding or combating a direct ground offensive elsewhere.

The air defence of the United Kingdom
The fluctuations of British policy are a microcosm of the changing priorities of air defence, set against the background of increasing integration of a national concern into a regional NATO one. Today the United Kingdom Air Defence Region (UKADR) is one of the four commands of the NATO Integrated Air Defence System. The Air Officer Commanding has the NATO title of 'C-in-C United Kingdom Air Forces' (UKAIR), subordinate to SACEUR, and responsible for a vital section of the western alliance's air defence structure. UKADR stretches in an arc 1500 km long from the north of the Faroes to the flanks of continental Europe, screening Soviet maritime approaches to the Atlantic.

The ground segment of Britain's air defences, the United Kingdom Air Defence Ground Environment (UKADGE), is fully integrated with NATO air defence and is being extensively upgraded, largely with US technology. The emphasis on dedicated interceptor aircraft and airborne early warning is stronger than ever before.

It was not always so. In the late 1960s Britain's defence planners effectively abandoned the idea of an anti-bomber radar defence line (having put the world's first such practical system into operation in 1939-40) and concentrated on a system which would drive off unwelcome reconnaissance or electronic intruders, such as Soviet Tu-142 Bears, rather than preparing to intercept an increasingly unlikely high- or medium-level, nuclear-armed bomber offensive. At the same time long-range surface-to-air missile defence of sites in the United Kingdom, other than nuclear deterrent bomber bases, became nominal.

In the early 1970s the emphasis switched to air defence against a perceived conventional bombing

The F-15 Eagle is replacing ageing F-106s in the air defence of the continental United States, while two Wings so far are forward-deployed in Europe.

threat. The shape of British air defence was recast, with the construction of new radar installations, the integration of civilian radars, and the flying of standing patrols in airborne early warning aircraft—in the first place using elderly Shackletons fitted with radars from Gannet carrier-based airborne early-warning aircraft which had been withdrawn from service. Control centres were decentralized to make them less vulnerable to attack, and several squadrons of point-defence Lightnings were retained. Phantoms, replaced in the strike role by Jaguars, were progressively assigned to the interceptor role, and the RAF wrote a special and highly expensive requirement for an air defence variant (ADV) of the Tornado multi-role combat aircraft, the first of which, armed with Skyflash air-to-air missiles, was due to enter service in 1985 as the Tornado F Mk 2. Then, beginning in the late 1970s, an extensive series of electronic improvements to UKADGE were put in hand, in order to fill gaps in the system, to strengthen the vital northern end covering the exits into the Atlantic, and to introduce the most modern data processing equipment so as to lessen reaction time and prepare for the integration of the Nimrod AEW force. The capacity of UKADGE has to be such as to be able to cope with the massive influx of US aircraft to their standby bases, to reinforce NATO in time of need.

The RAF's home-based air power—the radars of UKADGE, the missiles protecting airbases, the Air Defence Operations Centre at High Wycombe, and the sector stations at Buchan, Bulmer and Neatishead—are the operational concerns of Strike Command. No. Eleven Group, Strike Command, with its headquarters near the old Fighter Command HQ at Stanmore, in northwest London, has the task of actually maintaining sovereignty in no less than a million cubic miles of airspace. To carry out this task No. Eleven Group disposes of the following forces—some 65 Phantom FGR 2s and FG 1s of Nos 43 and 111 Squadron at Leuchars, Scotland, 29 Squadron and 228 Operational Conversion Unit at Coningsby, Lincolnshire, and No. 56 Squadron, based at Wattisham. Two Lightning squadrons, Nos 5 and 11, are based at Binbrook, and 24 more of these veteran interceptors are in reserve. In time of tension some of the force will be dispersed, singly or in pairs, to satellite airfields such as Stornaway on the Isle of Lewis.

The Tornado F Mk 2 is expected eventually to re-equip seven squadrons of Eleven Group. The F Mk 2 will carry the powerful Foxhunter air-intercept radar and be armed with a mixture of Skyflash and AIM-9L Sidewinder missiles, plus a rotary cannon. Ultimately, the air-to-air armament will be AMRAAM and ASRAAM. Two UK-based Phantom squadrons will be run on until the end of the decade, while the Lightnings will be phased out. Two Victor tanker units, with 16 front-line aircraft, will be joined by a squadron of nine converted VC-10s in the in-flight

Left: The Tornado F.2 was developed as an 'air defence variant' of the multi-role combat aircraft armed with Skyflash missiles and a Mauser cannon. 125 are on order for the RAF.

Below: Air defence at the sharp end—an RAF Phantom of No. 23 Squadron on quick reaction alert at RAF Stanley scrambling to police Falkland Islands airspace.

Binbrook ◉ ▲ North Coates
Scampton ◉
Waddington ◉ ◉ Coningsby
Barkston Heath ▲
West Raynham ★
Cottesmore ◉ ▲
Marham ◉ Coltishall ◉
Wittering ◉
Mildenhall ★
Alconbury ★◉▲ ★ Lakenheath
Wyton ◉ Honington
Wattisham◉▲ ★ Bentwaters
Bawdsey ▲ Woodbridge
★ Upper Heyford
◉ Brize Norton
London◉

SAM defence of Eastern England
▲ Bloodhound SAM site
★ USAF base
◉ RAF base

refuelling role. Six Vulcans were converted to in-flight tankers during the Falklands campaign and the RAF is exploring the use of Tristar wide-body airliners in the tanker role. Ground-attack Harrier G.R.3s of the RAF were also hastily modified during the South Atlantic fighting to carry AIM-9L Sidewinders on their outer wing pylons and proved effective air defence 'fighters', technically besting much faster and more capable opposition. The spirit of improvisation is also evident in the RAF's plans to arm more than 70 Hawk trainers with late-model Sidewinder air-to-air missiles for daylight point defence, the aircraft being drawn from tactical weapons units and training schools in Support Command.

Outside UKADR, two Phantom squadrons, Nos. 19 and 92, are assigned to RAF Germany, based at Wildenrath, while another squadron, No. 23, is based at RAF Port Stanley in the Falklands, acutely conscious of the problem of maintaining airspace sovereignty with slender resources. Fifteen ex-US Navy F-4Js are on order to replace this squadron in UK air defence, to be based at Wattisham. The Tornado ADV will not be based in Germany until the Phantoms are retired in the late 1980s.

Bloodhound surface-to-air missiles of No. 85 Squadron are based at Bawdsey, North Coates, Wyton, Barkston Heath, West Raynham and Wattisham, while shorter-range Rapiers of the RAF Regiment defend Leuchars and Lossiemouth. The Bloodhound units will form a line protecting RAF and USAF bases in eastern Britain from attack from the east and northeast. In addition, USAF bases at

Alconbury, Bentwaters, Fairford, Lakenheath, Mildenhall, Upper Heyford and Woodbridge will have Blindfire Rapier low-level SAM defence manned by the RAF regiment (see map).

The United Kingdom Air Defence Ground Environment forms a part of the much larger NADGE, the NATO air defence ground environment screen. NADGE watches the skies from the Norwegian North Cape to Sicily, then turns through Thrace, stretching to eastern Turkey, once again meeting the Soviet border. The original network was started in 1960, funded by 14 nations with the United States meeting just under one-third of the cost and providing much of the technology. As completed, it comprised some 47 radars and 37 computer centres, capable of detecting intruders up to 11,000 ft, but was vulnerable to low-altitude penetration and simple outflanking, although subsequently the separate UKADGE and Spanish *Combate Grande* systems were added to it, effectively pinning down its edges.

The system was substantially improved in 1975 and once again in the early 1980s was undergoing extensive electronic updating under the so-called Air Defence Ground Environment Integration segment (AEGIS) programme, which includes the NATO AWACS force. After a long period of political wrangling, the first of 18 Boeing E-3A Sentry Airborne warning and control aircraft systems (AWACS) became operational with the multinational NATO Early Warning Command in 1982. The aircraft are in fact registered in Luxembourg, which does not have an air force. They will be joined by the first of 11 RAF Nimrod AEW.3 aircraft in 1984.

Updated ground radars have been introduced by the Netherlands (1976), Italy (1977), Belgium (1980), Norway (1981), Britain and West Germany. The French Strida II system, while autonomously controlled, is compatible with the NATO system and contributes to the overall coverage.

The deep air defence of the German Federal Republic is closely integrated with the overall NADGE system. GEADGE (German Air Defence Ground Environment) is centred on the US Air Weapons Control System 412L, with seven sites linked by computer to the Combat Operations Center and is operated jointly by the United States, Britain and West Germany. The whole is a large defence complex which performs the functions of aerospace surveillance, identification and defence weapons control on NATO's vital central sector. If an aircraft intercept is ordered or a SAM launch commanded, AWCS 412L automatically computes and transmits the data necessary for an interception to be made. GEADGE, like other crucial assets in the NATO system, is undergoing an extensive updating programme and is supplemented by other mobile low-level radars.

The air defence of NATO

GEADGE is responsible for the electronic watch on NATO's most vital defence region, in essence the

Below: The veteran Lightning will continue in RAF service until the end of the decade, with two squadrons based at Binbrook. This aircraft features over-wing ferry fuel tanks and a low-visibility paint scheme.

Above: Wash down for a No. 23 Squadron Phantom at RAF Stanley. The RAF is acquiring 15 ex-US Navy F-4Js to plug the gap in UK air defence. Two Phantom squadrons will be retained with the RAF until the end of the 1980s.

Eleven BAe Nimrod airframes are being converted to AEW.3 airborne early-warning aircraft, replacing elderly Shackletons to electronically guard UK airspace.

German Federal Republic. The defence zone has precious little depth and even fewer natural barriers. Although this may not matter so much where air defence is concerned, NATO's general defence problem—having to overcome a Warsaw Pact force consisting of thousands of tactical aircraft—is bound up with the whole spectrum of counterair operations. At one end this is entirely defensive in outlook, but at the other envisages deep strikes against enemy airfields and is very close to the threshold of theatre nuclear war.

Because all-out conventional war is much more likely than any such attack on the United States (plus the need to contain it before resorting to nuclear weapons), the emphasis put by the USAF in Europe on active air defence is far greater than the strategic air defence of the continental United States.

The three component air forces of USAFE have a total of 35 fighter squadrons, providing in peacetime over 700 aircraft. A further 1500 USAF tactical aircraft could be deployed across the Atlantic to 73 colocated operating bases (COBs) within 30 days if necessary. Not all, of course, are dedicated counter-air fighters—and, meanwhile, all-weather air-superiority depends on the formidable capabilities of the F-15 Eagle, although there are currently only 90 in Europe, with a wing at Bitburg in West Germany and Camp New Amsterdam in the Netherlands. These aircraft have been subject to Multi-Stage Improvement Plans (MSIP) bringing them up to F-15C/D standard, with conformal fuel tanks and improved radar. An additional wing may supplant two F-4D squadrons at Spangdahlem, West Germany. The General Dynamics F-16 Fighting Falcon, also entering service with the air forces of the Netherlands, Belgium, Norway and Denmark, was originally conceived as a relatively simple fair-weather air combat fighter, but eventually emerged as a sophis-

ticated dual-capable strike aircraft in its own right.

The first USAFE F-16 wing was formed at Hahn, West Germany, in 1982, the second at Torrejón, Spain, in 1983. A third is scheduled to be formed at Ramstein, West Germany, in 1986, with the F-16s replacing F-4s in each case. In spite of the fact that some Phantoms are nearly 20 years old, a proportion will be retained until the late 1980s.

While the F-16 does not have the F-4's Sparrow radar-guided missile capability, the advent of AMRAAM on the F-16 in the late 1980s should redress any medium-range shortfall.

NATO's active air defence squadrons come under the command of the Supreme Allied Commander Europe (SACEUR), who is also responsible for the air defence of the United Kingdom. Europe-wide NATO disposes of some 3500 tactical aircraft, based on about 200 standard airfields, with the heaviest concentrations within Allied Command Central Europe (AFCENT). Allied Air Forces Northern Europe (AFNORTH) has assigned Danish and Norwegian forces, plus two West German air wings. Allied Forces Southern Europe (AFSOUTH) has an overall air command (Airsouth) for Greek, Italian and Turkish air forces, backed up by US carrier forces. The vital central sector is defended by two tactical air forces drawn up from US, British, Dutch, Belgian and Canadian squadrons commanded by Allied Air Forces Central Europe (AAFCE). Under the terms of the postwar peace, the RAF and USAF are responsible for maintaining the sovereignty of West German airspace and the integrity of the three air corridors to West Berlin. (France also shares responsibility for access to Berlin but does not contribute aircraft.) Only in the event of war would the Luftwaffe's interceptor wings be called upon.

Within West German territory and running parallel to the frontier is the Air Defence Identification Zone (ADIZ), in which only authorized flights are permitted. Investigation of intruders is the responsibility of the battle flight based at RAF Wildenrath,

RAF air defence Tornado F.2s are expected ultimately to equip seven squadrons, but will not be based in Germany until the Phantoms are retired at the end of the 1980s.

consisting of one Phantom from each of the two squadrons, plus the F-15 Eagles of the 32nd Tactical Fighter Squadron of the USAF based at Soesterberg in the Netherlands. On constant alert, the battle flights can be scrambled from their perpetually manned hardened shelters in under five minutes.

NATO close-range air defence

Ground-based air defence was one of the critical areas agreed on in 1978 by NATO governments to be reviewed under the Long-Term Defense Program and, in the face of Soviet Frontal Aviation's rapidly expanding capabilities, it was found to be wanting.

The large numbers of the US-developed Improved Hawk surface-to-air missile, subsequently deployed by most NATO nations, plus the NADGE radar screen, now represent perhaps the most closely knit and responsive of Supreme Allied Command Europe's defence assets on the central sector. Shortages identified in the 1978 review were made up and all Hawk batteries now have their basic load, together with increased stocks of standby rounds to hand, plus more of the all-important maintenance personnel.

The nuclear-tipped Nike Hercules SAM, developed in the early 1960s for barrier defence against high-flying aircraft, is still deployed by some NATO armed

BAe Hawk trainers armed with Sidewinder AAMs will provide back-up, daylight point defence of UK targets. This Hawk also carries a Sea Eagle anti-ship missile.

USAF operators watch the screen inside the shelter van of a TPS-43E mobile tactical radar. RAF Vulcans attacked a similar Argentinian air defence radar in the Falklands fighting.

forces but will be progressively replaced by the conventionally armed Patriot missile, which is far more effective and responsive against the much more likely low-level and cruise missile threat.

Early inter-NATO plans to deploy a Europe-wide Patriot belt have foundered, and the United States has had to enter into bilateral agreements with those countries who can afford it. France seems likely to develop its own missile, but in late 1983 the West Germans were able to enter into an agreement with the United States, by which the Roland short-range SAM would be deployed to protect three US air bases in Germany, to be manned by Luftwaffe personnel. In return the United States would provide 14 out of 28 Patriot fire units for West German air defence.

Western nations have developed a wide variety of short-range systems—guns and missiles, both towed and self-mobile, to strike back at tactical aircraft. There are also several equivalents of the Soviet shoulder-fired SA-7 anti-aircraft missile, which gives the infantryman a chance of defending himself or at least of robbing an attack of precision.

Close-range missile systems in service with Western armies include the British Rapier SAM, both in towed and tracked variants, with the option of Blindfire all-weather radar guidance.

The equivalent French Crotale system consists of a surveillance radar vehicle controlling up to three combined-launch and command-guidance vehicles. The missile itself is highly capable and can function in all weathers, with a maximum engagement range of up to 11 km and has been supplied to South Africa (as the Cactus) and to Saudi Arabia (as the Shahine), while there is also a naval version. The Italian Spada and Japanese Tansam are equivalent point-defence surface-to-air missile systems, which can be emplaced and made ready for action very rapidly.

At the time the potent Soviet ZSU-23-4 multiple anti-aircraft cannon on a tracked chassis appeared in 1965 there was no direct Western equivalent. The US Army acquired the Vulcan air-defence system in 1967, with a rotary Gatling cannon on a tracked vehicle, but the original radar did not have the contemporary Soviet weapon's search-and-track capabilities. Western European armies meanwhile responded with a range of tracked and wheeled mobile air defence systems mounting radar-guided guns and missiles, while the United States is only just now catching up.

The Roland, for example, jointly developed by France and West Germany, is a tube-launched missile which can be mounted on a range of armoured or soft-skin vehicles, and seemed set to become an important standardized weapon within NATO. A big programme to develop the weapon on a tracked quadruple launcher for the US Army was, however, cut back to a single light battalion to operate with the

Rapid Deployment Force. Meanwhile, experimental tests have been carried out, with four of the much smaller heat-seeking Stinger missiles being fired from each Roland launch cell. The Swedish RBS 70 SAM can be mounted on tracked or Land Rover-sized vehicles and fired while on the move, and the tracked Rapier made its operational debut with the British army in 1983. The Chapparal mobile air defence system, in US and Israeli service, is in essence a tracked quadruple launcher for ground-to-air versions of the Sidewinder air-to-air, heat-seeking missile. The system has been developed considerably since production first started in 1966 and now features autonomous IFF (identification of friend or foe) equipment and all-weather capability by means of radar tracking and command guidance.

Chapparal operates tactically in concert with the Vulcan rotary cannon, but this weapon will be eventually replaced by the new Sergeant York DIVAD (Division Air Defence) gun system. The system comprises a tracked vehicle mounting twin Bofors 40-mm guns in a turret liberally supplied with sensors and radar-guided fire control equipment to provide forward US Army forces with defence against tactical helicopters and ground-attack aircraft. The radar, in fact, is developed from the F-16 fighter's fire-control system and is backed up by the commander's and gunner's optical sights, which can override the automatic target engagement sequence if necessary. In full automatic engagement, the search radar detects and the fire control computer classifies and assigns priority to multiple targets. The tracking

radar automatically locks on and tracks the target, while the fire-control system selects the ammunition and opens fire when the target is in range. The guns fire prefragmented rounds, each with 640 tungsten spheres for ripping through aircraft structures.

Similar high-mobility anti-aircraft gun platforms (but without the high level of automated sophistication) include the French AMX-30 SA and the West German Gepard Flakpanzer which has twin 35-mm radar-controlled guns and is operated by West Germany, France, Switzerland and the Netherlands. The similar British Falcon project, which lacked radar for surveillance or ranging, was abandoned in the mid-1970s.

Virtually all armies deploy large numbers of light anti-aircraft guns and cannon which can be towed into position and brought into action very quickly. Indeed, a barrage of ground fire of whatever calibre is an instinctive response of the infantryman under attack and may cause even the most determined pilot to break off and miss the target.

In the Falklands fighting all losses of British fixed-wing aircraft (five Harriers) were officially attributed to ground fire. In fact, infantrymen blazed away with anything to hand at low-flying aircraft and fire from British general-purpose machine guns (GPMG) claimed at least one Argentinian Skyhawk. The South Atlantic campaign also showed up the shortcomings and underlined the strengths of several modern

An Airborne Warning and Control System (AWACS) acts as a force multiplier, maximizing warning times and the effectiveness of interceptors. This is one of NATO's 18 E-3A Sentries.

Above: The Improved Hawk surface-to-air missile will remain the mainstay of US and NATO field air defence until replaced by the Patriot system.

Main picture: The US Patriot is an advanced land mobile SAM which could ultimately replace Hawk and nuclear tipped Nike-Hercules in NATO air defence if funding allows.

Above: The British Rapier SAM proved itself in the Falklands fighting in spite of some operational shortcomings. This battery has the Blindfire tracking radar (foreground), giving the system an all-weather and night capability.

An Armée de l'Air C-135F tanker prepares to tank Mirage F.1s armed with Magic heat-seeking AAMs and Matra R530 medium-range missiles.

air defence weapons, and, by implication, their equivalents in service with other armies. The optically guided Rapier SAM was judged to have acquitted itself well and proved to be the 'hittile' the designers claimed it would be, downing 11 Argentinian aircraft. It took a long time, however, to set up the batteries (up to a day and a half), and of the 12 sets of equipment landed, five were badly shaken up by their voyage and needed major servicing before they could be used.

The Blowpipe shoulder-fired missile worked well in the hands of trained men, but it required skill and determination to gain its full effect. Blowpipe is unusual as a man-portable weapon in being command-guided—once it has been fired, the operator directs the missile to the target by means of a thumb-operated controller and a radio link. In contrast to heat seekers, therefore, which will lock on to a hot jet exhaust, Blowpipe works best in head-on engagements. In the Falklands, however, most were tail-chasing. The missile was not as robust as the soldiers thought it might be, but it claimed eight planes, primarily relatively slow, propeller-driven Pucara ground-attack aircraft. In Argentinian hands,

the missile is reported to have scored against several British helicopters.

Blowpipe is certainly heavy and a number of lighter US Stinger heat-seeking missiles were in the hands of the British SAS, but their performance was apparently disappointing. One claimed a Pucara but others went off in search of the nearest big heat source—a field kitchen in one case and a warship's funnel in another.

After the initial invasion the Argentines rapidly deployed an air defence system including a US-built TPS-43 air defence radar. It was sited on high ground and gave the defenders an invaluable overall tactical picture of enemy intentions and air movements. This was the target of repeated raids by RAF Vulcans armed with Shrike anti-radiation missiles, although they failed to put it out of action for longer than 45 minutes. The Argentines also had Roland SAMs, British short-range Tigercat SAMs and the West German Fledermaus anti-aircraft fire-control system, although US reports claim that none of the Rolands fired at Vulcans, Sea Harriers and other aircraft hit their target. The Tigercats were apparently more successful.

In complete contrast to the rigours of launching a missile from the shoulder at an oncoming attack aircraft is a system under development in the United

Above left: Mirage F.1s, examples of the primary French interceptor. French air defence has four regions, with headquarters at Metz, Paris, Bordeaux and Aix-en-Provence.
Above: The Mirage 2000, deliveries of which began in 1983, will give the Armée de l'Air an advanced Mach 2 plus interceptor, carrying R550 Magic and longer-range Matra Super 530 AAMs.

States which requires no human intervention whatsoever. The Self-Initiated Anti-Aircraft Missile (SIAM) programme is just that—a missile which can be emplaced around important point-defence sites and can fire itself automatically to intercept any enemy aircraft. SIAM is launched when a target is sensed. A dual mode seeker in the nose, combining radar and infrared sensors, hunts through the entire hemisphere above it until it finds a hostile target and locks on to it. The main motor ignites and the SIAM streaks off to impact. The system is being developed for land and sea use and, technically, could be employed to rapidly create 'aerial minefields' of self-activating missiles, over which aircraft would fly low only at their peril.

Soviet tactical air defence

The preceding chapter on tactical air power looked in detail at the formidable offensive capabilities of Soviet Frontal Aviation. Indeed, it was the shift from short-range defensive aircraft to long-ranging and highly capable offensive counterair and ground-attack aircraft in the 1970s and the technological leap that went with them that so alarmed the West. A Tactical Air Army of Frontal Aviation is integrated into the Soviet military command structure at the 'front' level, providing the air power for a number of combined-arms armies and varies in size according to the importance of the area to which it is assigned. The 16th FA Army, covering the crucial group of Soviet forces in East Germany, numbers more than 1000 aircraft, whereas others in military districts within the Soviet Union number fewer than 100. Frontal Aviation exists very much as part of the combined arms concept, able to apply offensive shock power on a large scale. Heavy emphasis, however, has always been maintained on battlefield air defence, which means the deployment of large tactical counterair forces including interceptors, SAMs, and mobile guns and rockets in profusion. From the front line to a distance of 500 km within Warsaw Pact airspace, some 2350 air-to-air fighters would be available to oppose any NATO penetration.

The largest unit of an FA Army is the division (*divisiya*), while 'air defence cover' divisions (*prikry-*

tirie) function alongside those concerned with support, reconnaissance and so on. A division consists of three and sometimes more regiments (*polki*), each usually possessing three squadrons (*eskadrili*) of 16-18 aircraft, including a rotational reserve.

The function of the air defence squadrons is to provide cover for ground units and the tactical aircraft supporting them. According to published doctrine, when operating on the defensive, Soviet interceptors would normally be deployed at medium and high altitude, leaving low-altitude air defence to land-mobile gun and missile units. Frontal Aviation's primary air-to-air fighter is the MiG-23 (Flogger B and G), of which over 1500 are in service. Floggers are supplanting the long-serving MiG-21 Fishbeds which, although still deployed in large numbers, are expected to be finally withdrawn in the latter half of the 1980s. The primary air defence variants of this veteran short-range fighter are the late-model Fishbed-L and -N. The two versions of the Flogger differ in some aerodynamic details which, reportedly, give the later G-model more agility in air-to-air combat. Both variants mount a twin-barrel 23-mm GSh-231 cannon on the fuselage centreline and carry up to four air-to-air missiles on stations beneath each air intake trunk and the fixed inboard wing panel. The first generation air-to-air missile, the AA-2 Atoll, is still widely used, although a mix of AA-7 Apex semi-active radar homing medium-range missiles and AA-8 Aphid dogfight missiles with infrared homing is more usual. Both marks of Flogger can carry bombs or rocket packs in place of air-to-air missiles in their secondary ground-support role.

The MiG-23's maximum speed ranges from just over Mach 1 at sea level to well over twice the speed of sound at altitude without military stores. Typical combat radius with a drop tank on the centreline is around 600 mi. (960 km), but there is little margin for afterburning supersonic dash.

Land-based tactical air defence

Soviet combat doctrine recognizes that continuous air defence is an essential part of combined arms warfare, especially in the offensive role. The structure of Soviet air defence forces, the disposition of their forward runways, and the design of short-range air defence weapons and radars are optimized to be able to 'leapfrog' each other, providing a continuous shield for an advancing formation. Meanwhile, large numbers of highly mobile low-level air defence systems are designed to operate with armour on the move, such as the ZSU-23-4 quadruple radar-guided cannon and SA-8 Gecko surface-to-air missile on a high-mobility amphibious vehicle. The ZSU-23-4 (generally referred to as 'Zoos' in US flier's parlance) has been in service since 1965 and has been deployed in large numbers, giving Soviet armoured formations an autonomous counterweight to much of NATO's helicopter-gunship and A-10 tankbuster close-support fire power. The quadruple 23-mm guns are radar-guided and stabilized, able to fire on the move while spitting out high-explosive incendiary and armour-piercing incendiary bullets at 200 rounds per

Above: Drone helicopter provides a target for multiple gunfire from the US Army's Divad Sergeant York mobile anti-aircraft gun system.

Below: ADATS is a joint US-Swiss project for a dual purpose anti-tank, anti-aircraft missile system with advanced target acquisition and guidance systems.

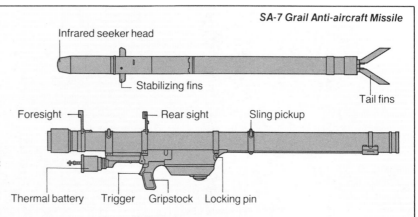

SA-7 Grail

One of the most famous of contemporary weapons, the SA-7, codenamed 'Grail' by NATO, is in very wide service with Soviet bloc and client armed forces. Simple and durable, the SA-7 is a man-portable, shoulder-fired anti-aircraft missile employing infrared guidance. It is effective only in a stern chase against low-flying aircraft, especially helicopters, and it has been officially assessed with a range of up to ten km.

Simple optical sighting and tracking are used – the seeker becoming active when the operator has acquired the target. When the seeker itself has locked on, an indicator light tells the operator to fire the missile.

Early model SA-7s were vulnerable to simple countermeasures such as flares but later versions are fitted with filters to screen out decoys.

SA-7 Grail Anti-aircraft Missile

Infrared seeker head
Stabilizing fins
Tail fins
Foresight
Rear sight
Sling pickup
Thermal battery
Trigger
Gripstock
Locking pin

barrel per minute, normally firing in bursts of 50 rounds per barrel.

Advanced optical sights, a fire control computer and moving target indicator make it very accurate and able to engage aircraft while itself moving at 25 km an hour. There are, however, drawbacks. The guns have a tendency to fire inadvertently when the turret is traversing, they overheat and the radar cannot engage targets below 200 ft.

Nevertheless NATO tactical doctrine affords the Zoos top priority, to be neutralized as quickly as possible before other armoured vehicles are engaged, whether by helicopters firing TOWs from extreme range on the flanks or by direct ground fire.

Air defence officers are attached to all headquarters down to regimental level. At Front and Army level, there are separate Air Defence Commander and his staff working alongside general headquarters. Centralized control on this rung of the command ladder co-ordinates the efforts of the interceptor aircraft of Frontal Aviation and the brigades of area defence surface-to-air missiles with the point-defence efforts of manoeuvre units actually in the field.

The divisional army air defence commander is in charge of the division's air defence efforts, which excludes aircraft but includes point-defence SAMs, anti-aircraft guns and mobile radars, while also establishing the priority of the points to be defended.

Soviet doctrine normally assigns highest priority to protecting nuclear-capable systems, followed by headquarters, assembly areas and key geographical choke-points such as river crossings. Tank and motor rifle formations have their own self-mobile anti-aircraft batteries.

The Soviets have no illusions about the effectiveness of NATO tactical air power and about how vulnerable mass formations being funnelled through West German choke points would be. The answer is to deploy air defence weapons throughout an army sector—the fighters of Frontal Aviation would fly below an altitude of four km at their peril, because this is where the army's own defence umbrella begins.

In fact area SAM defence, fighter cover and divisional short-range point defence are all designed to interlock in their zones of effectiveness. In the 1973 Middle East war, Israeli aircraft that got below the medium-range SA-6 missiles were mauled by ZSU-23-4 mobile multiple cannon. If they got above the SA-6s, they would be driven back into the killing zone by long-range area-defence SAMs. The same principle applies to radars; if a Fan Song SA-2 fire-control radar loses the target in ground clutter, a Low Blow system, which has been especially designed to work at low altitude, will pick it up.

At the other end of the scale is the SA-7 Grail, a shoulder-launched heat-seeking SAM, issued as a self-defence weapon to motor rifle platoons. Although the debut of that missile in the Vietnam war rendered obsolete at a stroke the whole class of low-technology counter insurgency (COIN) aircraft, its combat effectiveness in warfare between the superpowers is questionable. Some 5000 SA-7s were launched in the 1973 Middle East war, to claim only two Israeli aircraft, while others were slightly damaged. The poor results were due to the missile's less than lethal warhead, its susceptibility to quite simple counter-measures and the fact that, unlike the British

The US Chapparal SAM is a straightforward adaptation of the heat-seeking Sidewinder air-to-air missile. This is the new air-transportable lightweight version.

Blowpipe, it could operate only by chasing from behind a target's main heat source, in effect a jet aircraft's tailpipe. It cannot overtake aircraft moving at more than 500 knots and will head off towards the sun if fired at an angle within 20° of that source of heat. It will even go for the surface of the earth if fired at an elevation less than 25°. The SA-7 is reportedly easy to outmanoeuvre and can be countered by dropping simple infrared decoy flares. Like many heat-seeking missiles, it can be thrown off if the aircraft simply climbs towards the sun and then quickly turns away, while the missile continues to fly towards the greatest heat source.

Soviet strategic air defence

The large numbers of interceptor aircraft available to Frontal Aviation and other Warsaw Pact air forces, plus the area-defence SAMs deployed in eastern Europe, represent a formidable outer bulwark for the air defence of the Soviet Union itself. In contrast to the attitude in the United States, the direct threats of bombers and cruise missiles to the homeland are taken extremely seriously and very large forces are dedicated to countering them. Indeed, an important reason for the US persistence with the cruise missile as a strategic weapon, in parallel with ballistic missiles, is to force the Soviets to keep up their spending on defence against so-called 'air-breathing threats', diverting money from offensive weapons programmes or anti-submarine warfare, for example. Defence against cruise missiles means a new generation of 'look-down shoot-down' missile, carrying inter-ceptors, airborne early warning and control aircraft, low-level radars and ultra-responsive surface-to-air missiles. It has even been reported that serious consideration is being given to the building of dummy landscapes for throwing cruise missiles off course.

Since 1948 the air defence of the Soviet homeland has been grouped as a separate command, the Voiska Protivovozdushnoy Oborony Strany—PVO-Strany. In contrast to US strategic defences, very large numbers of launchers, interceptor aircraft and radar sites are still deployed despite the long decline in US manned bomber strength. Efforts to develop anti-ballistic missile defences and satellite killers have also been strenuous, with PKO (anti-space defence) and PRO (anti-rocket defence) established as separate sub-organizations in the mid-1960s. PVO-Strany has 630,000 troops organized in ten air defence districts (with special emphasis on Moscow and the oil-producing centre of Baku), numerous air defence regiments and some 14 specialist schools.

The commander of PVO-Strany since 1978 is Marshal of Aviation Aleksandr Ivanovich Koldunov, a fighter ace of World War II, credited with bringing down 46 enemy aircraft. He commands the three basic components of the force—manned interceptor squadrons, radio technical troops and zenith rocket troops—and close ties are maintained between PVO units and civil defence troops.

The Radiotekhnicheskiye Voiska RTV or radio technical troops are responsible for the electronic watch of airspace, operating space systems and a dense and overlapping network of over 6000 radars. There are three and possibly four over-the-horizon backscatter, long-range air defence radar sites—near Minsk, near Nikolayev in the Caucasus, and in the Far East looking north towards the routes of entry over the Pole.

Anti-aircraft defence

During World War II the German Luftwaffe never developed a practical long-range strategic bombing aircraft able to hit Soviet industry evacuated east of the Ural mountains. The advocate of a 'Ural bomber' programme, Luftwaffe General Wever, was killed in a plane crash in 1938 and his plans died with him. Moscow and Soviet industrial centres never came under sustained strategic air attack, but when Soviet troops overran Dresden and Berlin in 1945 they saw just how devastating the long reach of RAF Bomber Command and the USAAF Eighth Air Force had been. The lesson was not lost and strategic air defence became a key postwar military priority. PVO-Strany was separated from the ground forces in 1948, the first MiG-15 jets were operational by 1949, and SA-1 SAMs were deployed in two huge concentric rings around Moscow by 1955. The much more capable SA-2 were deployed in a crash programme from 1962 onwards.

Today PVO-Strany deploys about 12,400 missile launchers at some 1400 fixed sites, together with 2250 interceptor aircraft, plus at least ten Moss AWACS warning and control aircraft, although these lack the ability to pick out targets from land 'clutter' or to effect low-level coverage over water. A new AWACS based on the Il-76 airframe, codenamed 'Mainstay', is entering service. Airborne early warn-ing, new interceptors and new missiles are part of the efforts to close the low-level gap. The first Soviet weapon identified as having a degree of anti-cruise missile capacity is the new SA-10, with a maximum speed of Mach 6 and a range of 50km. The system uses a tower-mounted surveillance radar to pick up low-flying targets. At present transportable SA-10 batteries are deployed in small numbers to protect high-value critical targets within the Soviet Union.

In addition, the air forces of the other Warsaw Pact countries have interceptor regiments and SAM sites mounting SA-2s and SA-3s. In early 1983 the construction was completed of a chain of SAM complexes mounting the 290-km range SA-5 missile, stretching the length of the European central front from the Baltic coast of East Germany to southern Czechoslovakia.

From Aug. 1978 onwards PVO-Strany appears to

Right: The Sergeant York air defence gun system uses twin 40-mm Bofors cannon with a fire control radar derived from the F-16 aircraft's APG AN/APG-66 system.

Right: AIM-7 Sparrow air-to-air missiles have an effective range up to 100 km, but require continuous radar illumination of the target by the launch aircraft. Before the missile's rocket motor fires, it is released out and down, as from this F-15 Eagle.

Below right: A USAF armourer in full NBC kit (Nuclear, Biological, Chemical) assembles an AIM-7 Sparrow inside an F-15's hardened aircraft shelter.

have been merged progressively with Army Air Defence, the Voiska Protivovozdushnoy Oborony Sukhoputnykh Voisk (PVO SK), which provides the tactical SAM defence of ground forces. By 1983 most of PVO Strany's air defence district HQs had been disbanded and their functions taken over by the Military District HQ. Currently, only five PVO-Strany District HQs remain; at Archangel, Kiev, Moscow, Sverdlovsk and Novossibirsk. The operational implications of this change are not yet clear. However, the destruction of the Korean Airlines flight KAL 007 in Aug. 1983 indicated just how seriously the Soviets take the enforcement of airspace sovereignty over critical strategic areas and how inflexible is Soviet operational doctrine which puts aircraft in the air under close control by the fighter directors at ground-control intercept stations.

Whatever the truth of the matter, according to Colonel General Romanov, the PVO-Strany chief of staff, an aircraft flying without navigation lights was detected entering Soviet airspace. An interceptor made contact at 30,000 ft and, according to Romanov's testimony, the intruder was assumed to be a US RC-135 electronic intelligence platform. The order to shoot it down apparently came from the commander of the Soviet Far East military region, who acted without consulting the political leaders in Moscow. The death of 360 civilians was the tragic result.

Manned interceptors

In the 1960s the air threat to the Soviet Union came from high-level bombers. The threat today comes from low-level penetrators and cruise missiles. Aircraft such as the Mach 3 MiG-25 Foxbat represent the response to the first threat: they are designed to get to high altitudes as fast as possible and launch large air-to-air missiles at long range. The bigger, slower Tupolev Tu-128 and Sukhoi Su-15 were designed to do the same thing at an even longer range. Numerically the most important interceptor in IAP-VO Strany Istrebitelnaya Aviatsiya (the interceptor fighter component of national air defence) is the MiG-23 Flogger B/G variable-geometry multirole fighter. The Flogger B with its 'High Lark' radar was described as the first Soviet aircraft with a demonstrated if rudimentary ability to track and engage targets flying below its own altitude.

This 'look-down' ability of a modern radar to distinguish moving targets seen from above against the background clutter of the ground itself is a vital prerequisite of defence against fast low-flying aircraft and cruise missiles. The second component is a 'shoot-down' missile that itself can seek out its target from above.

The Soviets are beginning to deploy aircraft with 'look-down-shoot-down' capability, notably the MiG 31 Foxhound (a two-seat Foxbat equipped with a highly capable radar), mounting AA-9 air-to-air missiles with semi-active radar and active radar terminal guidance.

In 1979 US sources reported a new fighter aircraft under development by the Mikoyan-Gurevich design bureau. It was designated Ram-L (Ramenskoye Type L) and later MiG-29 Fulcrum. Fulcrum is a multirole air-superiority aircraft but could function very efficiently in the interceptor role with the appropriate radar and new-generation 'look-down-shoot-down' missiles.

The air defence of the United States

A distinction should be made between the early warning systems developed by the US which guard against attack by ballistic missile and active defence aimed directly against penetrating aircraft. The early warning systems, such as the Ballistic Missile Early Warning System (BMEWS), are not there to direct a defence—the anti-missile systems do not exist to do so—but to ensure that the weapons of retaliation can be armed and launched in the few minutes before they are destroyed by an incoming attack and thus preserve the credibility of nuclear deterrence.

NORAD, North American Aerospace Defense Command, which is today responsible for ensuring the electronic missile watch, was jointly set up by the United States and Canada in the 1950s, in the days before intercontinental ballistic missiles, and at its

---

PVO Strany Interceptors

MiG-23 Flogger B/G
Over 800 of these fighter versions of the MiG-23 variable-geometry combat aircraft serve with PVO Strany. The United States is believed to have some supplied clandestinely by Egypt, against which simulated combat tests have been flown by aircraft and cruise missiles.

Flogger-B has J-band radar (NATO High Lark), with a range of 53 mi.

Flogger-G has a smaller dorsal fin.

Powerplant: 1 × Tumansky turbojet, 25,350 lb static thrust

Max speed: Mach 2·3 at altitude, Mach 1·1 at sea level

Combat radius: (600 mi.)

Armament: 23-mm twin-barrel cannon, AA-7 radar-guided and AA-8 heat-seeking AAMs.

MiG-25 Foxbat A
Some 240 of these high-powered interceptors are still operational with air defence forces, although numbers are slowly declining. The Foxbat revealed to the West in 1976 was not the superfighter it was purported to be, built mainly of steel and with a vacuum-tube technology radar.

Powerplant: 2 × Tumansky afterburning turbojets, each 24,350-lb static thrust

Max speed: Mach 2·8

Combat radius: (700 mi.)

Armament: 4 × AAMs, a mix of AA-6, -7, -8s.

peak controlled extensive networks of air defence radars, with large numbers of interceptor aircraft and missile forces at the disposal of Air Defense Command. The highly specialized interceptor aircraft of the period, such as the Convair F-102, F-106 and the all-weather McDonnell F-101B Voodoo, were even equipped with Genie and Nuclear Falcon nuclear-tipped air-to-air missiles, so seriously was the so-called 'bomber gap' scare of the period taken.

By 1960 there were 67 'active' or regular and 55 Air National Guard squadrons dedicated to air defence, backed up by seven Bomarc SAM squadrons. US Army-operated nuclear-tipped Nike Hercules missiles provided area defence of cities, with shorter-range Hawk missiles affording low-level cover.

The projected Soviet bomber threat, however, never materialized. Heavy bomber strength peaked at around 210 Bisons and Bears in 1966, then fell back to 140, the current total, before the appearance of the new generation of Soviet manned bombers. The 1000+ SAM batteries that once defended US cities were reduced to 100 by 1974 and disappeared entirely in 1979. Without missile defences and with the disbanding of Air Defense Command (Adcom) in 1980, therefore, the enforcement of US air sovereignty is the responsibility of Tactical Air Command, with its own Air Defense TAC (ADTAC) headquarters at Langley AFB, Florida, supported by the not inconsiderable resources of the Air National Guard. ADTAC maintains five air defence divisions and operates the USAF Air Defense Weapons Center at Tyndall AFB, Florida, which is the Air Force's

MiG-25 Foxbat, PVO-Strany's high performance interceptor did not turn out to be the wonder plane it once promised to be. A two-seat development codenamed Foxhound is entering service.

central technical development centre for all air defence weapons. ADTAC forces based in the north-eastern United States and Iceland regularly get 'live' practice intercepting Soviet Bear D reconnaissance aircraft approaching the eastern US seaboard and the Greenland-Iceland-UK (GIUK) gap.

Assigned interceptor aircraft total 261, not including the 54 CF-101 Voodoos of the Canadian Armed Forces (to be replaced by CF-118s). For over two decades the burden of air defence rested on Convair F-102s and F-106s, dating in design back to the 1950s, but now the very capable F-15 Eagle is progressively coming into service. As from spring 1984, four active and five Air National Guard squadrons could put up 153 F-106s. One active TAC squadron is operational with F-15s and one active squadron (57th FIS), under the control of C-in-C Atlantic and based in Iceland, operates F-4 Phantoms. The Air National Guard further operates five squadrons, totalling 90 F-4Cs and Ds. Alaskan Air Command has important air defence responsibilities and is converting two fighter squadrons from F-4E to F-15 Eagle. A total of 1472 Eagles is planned for USAF service, while orders to date amount to 756. Air defence forces can be augmented, as the need arises, from other assigned TAC units and from naval and marine air forces.

ADTAC has responsibility for support of the Distant

Early Warning (DEW) line of radar stations that crosses the extreme north of Canada, watching for Soviet aircraft incursions from over the Pole. While much of the original network of radar sites guarding approaches to the United States has disappeared, the DEW line has been retained. Its capabilities have been enhanced in a programme called 'Seek Igloo' and its information is fed directly to the NORAD Combat Operations Center. Plans to replace the DEW line with over-the-horizon backscatter radar (OTH-B) have been suspended, because of the technical difficulties in making such a system work in polar regions.

Two similar systems are in prototype stage, watching the approaches to the eastern and western seaboards with transmitter/receiver complexes based in Maine and in Washington state. Two further OTH-B installations for watching southern approaches are under consideration.

For 25 years the electronic watch on airspace within, and peripheral to, the continental United States rested on the so-called SAGE/BUIC system (semi-automatic ground environment/back-up interceptor control system). The last six of the original 20 sites were replaced in 1983 by a new network, called Joint Surveillance System (JSS), which involves Canadian participation and joint provision of radars and data by the USAF and civil Federal Aviation Authority. The JSS will eventually control 84 radars (46 in the United States, 14 in Alaska and 24 in Canada) from seven so-called 'Region Operations Control Centers' (ROCCs). One of the JSS sensors is the balloon-borne radar based at Cudjoe Key, Florida, called Seek Skyhook, which specifically provides coverage in the direction of Cuba.

The function of the ROCCs is to process data on air traffic movements, identify potential threats and direct interceptor aircraft where necessary, while also passing information direct to NORAD. In time of war the 'soft' ROCC centres would pass on their function to E-3A AWACS aircraft, which can conduct target identification and intercept operations from the air. Of the planned total of 34 E-3As, six are assigned in peacetime to air defence and are operated by the 552nd Airborne Warning and Control Wing TAC, based at Tinker AFB, Oklahoma. Squadrons from the wing are rotated to three bases within the United States, together with Okinawa, and Keflavik AFB, Iceland. The Keflavik E-3As provide in-depth coverage of the Atlantic approaches to the United States, while the later models (E-3Bs) will also have the ability to detect low-level intruders over water.

Above right: In contrast to the United States the Soviet Union deploys a very large force for the air defence of the homeland. The Tupolev Tu-114 Moss airborne early warning aircraft, however, is far less sophisticated than its US counterpart, although a new Soviet AWACs aircraft is reported to be entering service. *Below:* Over 1000 MiG-21 Fishbed variants remain in service as the primary air superiority aircraft of Frontal Aviation.

CHAPTER 3

Combat Helicopters

The rotor wing aircraft is not an ideal military platform. It is noisy, it vibrates, it is thirsty for fuel and requires a lot of maintenance. Its rotor and dynamic train are vulnerable to hits and mechanical breakdown, and it is also far slower than its fixed-wing counterparts. But, taken in the context of land warfare, with the helicopter understood as a super-fast and super-mobile vehicle rather than an agile, if slow aircraft, then its true impact on land warfare can be fully appreciated. In 20 years the helicopter has evolved from a flying bus for infantry into a formidable combat machine in its own right, able to fly to and fight at the heart of the battlefield, lavishly equipped with target-acquisition systems, guns and missiles and with a thick defensive hide. The purpose-designed attack helicopter, however, as exemplified by the US Army's Hughes AH-64 Apache, is an extremely expensive military asset both to acquire and to maintain. To justify this expense it must be able to deal with a large amount of enemy armour, while surviving ground fire and even survive in helicopter-to-helicopter combat. Armour protection against shell hits, twin engines and back-up duplicate systems are today considered essential aids to 'survivability', although some would argue that the only way for a helicopter to survive is not to be hit in the first place.

However, this in turn calls for exceptional manoeuvrability in a wide speed band and at low level, where trees and hills may provide natural cover similar to that found in street fighting, but such things

as electricity pylons also wait as deadly snares. There were only three such aerial cables in the Falklands but military helicopters managed to run into all of them. How different it might be in West Germany.

These so-called 'nap of the earth' flying techniques require enormous skill from the pilots and the aid of advanced night vision and adverse weather equipment in order to be able to operate and engage armour in just the conditions the enemy may choose in which to commit ground forces. It is no use investing huge amounts in a tank-killing helicopter defence line if it will not work in the rain!

These problems have led to two divergent approaches in the story of the attack helicopter outlined in this chapter—the super-capable purpose-designed weapons platform and the relatively cheap conversion of a standard helicopter, which goes right back to the way that armed helicopters began. The armed helicopter as a concept is barely 30 years old. The French began in the early 1950s with improvised lash-ups in the war against the Vietminh in Vietnam. In another drawn-out colonial war—in the rugged terrain of Algeria—Sikorsky S-55s and Sud Alouettes flew with fixed forward-firing machine guns, rocket pods and, later, wire-guided missiles. In the context of fighting guerrillas the concept was judged highly successful.

In Korea the US Army and Marine Corps had fitted their first-generation helicopters with machine guns firing from side windows, while Marine Experimental Squadron HMX-1 was testing helicopters as early as 1949 with all sorts of ordnance, including even mortars and bombs.

By 1956-7 the US Army was actively developing

Armed helicopter experiments began in earnest in the early 1950s and matured in the Vietnam conflict. This US Army OH-6A mounts two M60 7·62 mm machine guns.

Above: Troop-carrying helicopters confer a degree of mobility on the battlefield which could transform traditional military operations. *Below:* Over 1000 UH-60A Blackhawks are on order for the US Army, which has demonstrated their operability in a wide range of environments, including the Egyptian desert.

A US Army anti-tank platoon scurries from their UH-60A. The US Army is the western world's largest operator of helicopters, with a fleet of some 8300 aircraft.

Above: This Hughes 500MD Defender of the Kenyan Army air force carries four TOW wire guided anti-tank missiles.

Below: More than 200 B105P anti-tank helicopters serve with the West German Army. Standard armament as here is six HOT wire-guided anti-tank missiles.

tactical doctrines for the concept of 'air cavalry' units —units that would be taken into battle with their own aerial fire support, not by wheel or track but by rotor. Meanwhile, volunteer pilots at the Army Aviation School began, from June 1956 onwards, to experiment with armed helicopters, taking aloft and firing everything from turret-mounted machine guns to recoilless rifles. In March 1958 the 7292nd Aerial Combat Reconnaissance (ACR) company was formed to bring in line the diverse units which had been conducting trials.

In 1962 the high-powered Army Tactical Mobility Requirements Board made its report and shaped the future of US Army flying around the new concepts of battlefield mobility which the helicopter made possible. The report boldly compared nascent rotorcraft development with the early days of fixed-wing flying and predicted a similar leap forward in real capabilities and combat power. It foresaw that transport helicopters would need to be escorted by armed helicopters, which would provide 'a mobile elevated platform for immediate and continuous fire support in mobile situations'. The report paved the way for the transformation of the ACR into the US Army's 1st Cavalry Division (Airmobile) and very soon this unit would be proving the concepts of rotor-borne battlefield mobility in Vietnam.

The jungle warfare of Vietnam was the nursery of the combat helicopter, although the special conditions of counter-insurgency warfare caused the

The US Army is reworking its 1000-strong fleet of AH-1 HueyCobra attack helicopters to AH-1S standard, equipped with TOW anti-tank missiles.

development to be slanted in a particular direction. The Bell UH-1 utility transport, the ubiquitous 'Huey', was by far the most widely used helicopter in the conflict. By 1966 there were no fewer than 1400 rotorcraft in Vietnam, most of them Hueys. From the beginning of US involvement the UH-1s were modified on the ground to carry weapons—being equipped in the first place with twin-fixed forward-firing machine guns and then with traversing M60 machine guns on fuselage outriggers. At the end of 1962 the first 20 armed UH-1s, with factory-fitted Emerson Electric turret-mounted M-60s and rocket racks, arrived in Vietnam. Even the standard troop-carrying assault UH-1s were temporarily equipped with M60s in each cabin door.

As air cavalry operations developed, the normal complement of a US Army UH-1 company was made up of nine armed UH-1s ('gunships' or 'hogs') and 16 unarmed troop carriers ('slicks').

In the early days of operations in Vietnam the gunship helicopters would arrive over the landing zone minutes before the main body and shoot up the area with suppressive fire and rockets. The troop-carrying helicopters were, in fact, lighter and more vulnerable than their armed sister ships. The 'hogs' were a good ten miles an hour slower and, if they left formation to attack a target, could not catch up.

At the beginning of 1963 the US Army announced its requirement for a purpose-designed convoy escort and suppressive fire platform. In fact the manufacturers were already ahead of the game, Bell having produced a mock-up of a combat UH-1 in June 1962. It was called the Iroquois Warrior, and featured just

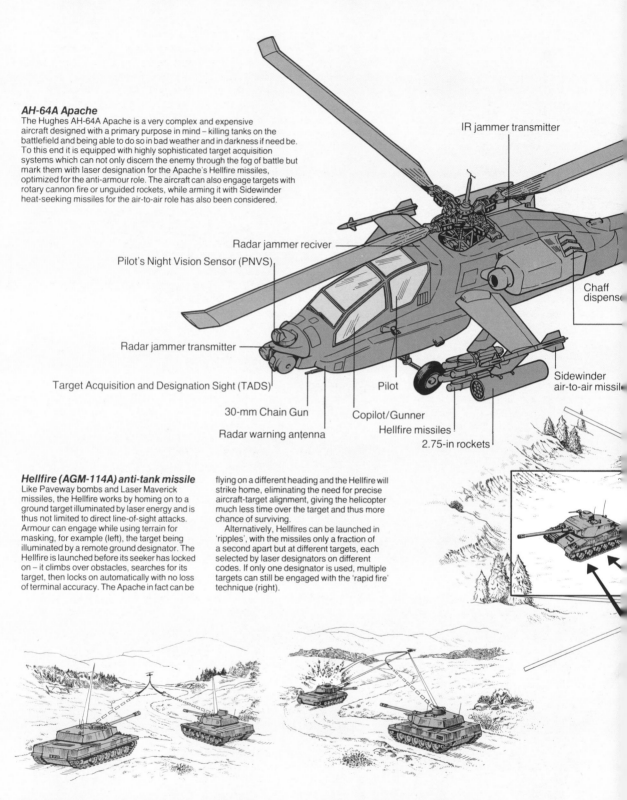

AH-64A Apache

The Hughes AH-64A Apache is a very complex and expensive aircraft designed with a primary purpose in mind – killing tanks on the battlefield and being able to do so in bad weather and in darkness if need be. To this end it is equipped with highly sophisticated target acquisition systems which can not only discern the enemy through the fog of battle but mark them with laser designation for the Apache's Hellfire missiles, optimized for the anti-armour role. The aircraft can also engage targets with rotary cannon fire or unguided rockets, while arming it with Sidewinder heat-seeking missiles for the air-to-air role has also been considered.

IR jammer transmitter

Radar jammer reciver

Pilot's Night Vision Sensor (PNVS)

Chaff dispenser

Radar jammer transmitter

Target Acquisition and Designation Sight (TADS)

Pilot

Sidewinder air-to-air missile

30-mm Chain Gun

Copilot/Gunner

Radar warning antenna

Hellfire missiles

2.75-in rockets

Hellfire (AGM-114A) anti-tank missile

Like Paveway bombs and Laser Maverick missiles, the Hellfire works by homing on to a ground target illuminated by laser energy and is thus not limited to direct line-of-sight attacks. Armour can engage while using terrain for masking, for example (left), the target being illuminated by a remote ground designator. The Hellfire is launched before its seeker has locked on – it climbs over obstacles, searches for its target, then locks on automatically with no loss of terminal accuracy. The Apache in fact can be

flying on a different heading and the Hellfire will strike home, eliminating the need for precise aircraft-target alignment, giving the helicopter much less time over the target and thus more chance of surviving.

Alternatively, Hellfires can be launched in 'ripples', with the missiles only a fraction of a second apart but at different targets, each selected by laser designators on different codes. If only one designator is used, multiple targets can still be engaged with the 'rapid fire' technique (right).

Ripple Fire Hellfire Launch with Ground designation

Autonomous Rapid-Fire Hellfire Launch

Radar warning antenna

Flare dispenser

Radar warning antenna

Infrared emission supressor

Key to the Apache's all-weather combat capability is the target acquisition designation sight (TADS) and the pilot night vision sensor (PNVS). TADS provides the gunner with a search, detection and recognition capability using direct view optics, television, or forward-looking infrared (FLIR), which can be used singly or together depending on circumstances.

Once acquired, targets can be tracked manually or automatically for attack with rockets, the 30 mm cannon or by laser-guided Hellfire missiles. The laser may also be used to designate targets for attack by other helicopters

or for other laser-guided systems. The TADS is mounted in a rotating turret in the nose housing the sensors, coupled to the co-pilot/gunner's position via an optical relay tube.

The PNVS is used by the pilot for night navigation and consists of a FLIR sensor system mounted above the TADS, an electronics unit and the pilot's display and controls. The system is co-ordinated with the pilot's helmet display and provides imagery, allowing the Apache to be flown in a 'nap of the earth' profile around ground obstructions while also producing target information if necessary.

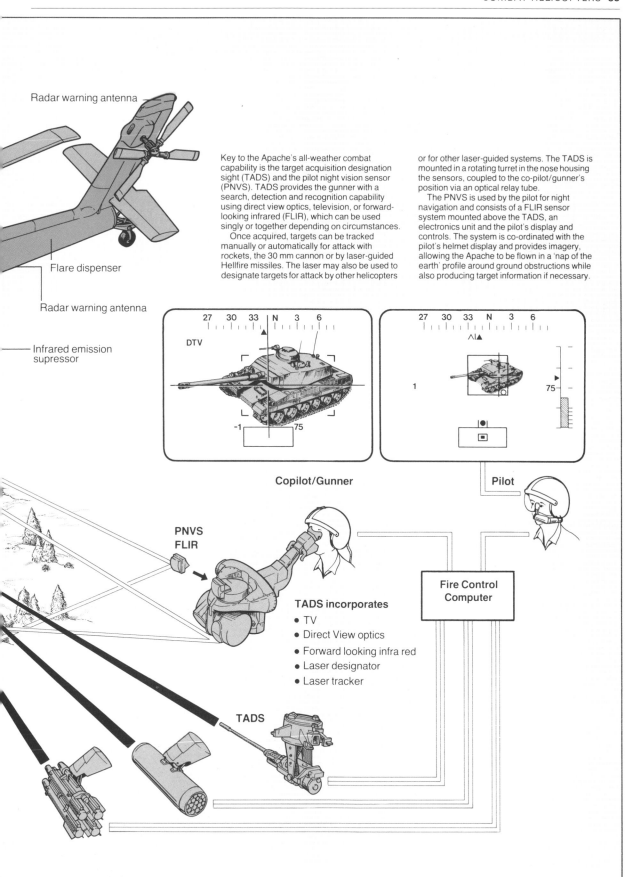

DTV

Copilot/Gunner

Pilot

PNVS
FLIR

TADS incorporates
- TV
- Direct View optics
- Forward looking infra red
- Laser designator
- Laser tracker

Fire Control Computer

TADS

two crew members in stepped tandem cockpits. It had a small frontal area, stub wings and a purposeful-looking airframe, and presaged the shape of a whole new class of combat aircraft. Getting a prototype into the air to impress the Army took longer. Kaman produced an armed land-attack version of their Seasprite shipborne helicopter and Bell got a heavily modified Model 47 into the air as the Sioux Scout in 1963.

The US Army, meanwhile, was refining its requirement and demanding more of the technology in its concept, now defined as the Advanced Aerial Fire Support System (AAFSS). It called for a top speed of no less than 260 mph and a ten-minute hover in its main mission profile—all of this with heavy armament. The AAFSS concept was stretching technology to the limits, but meanwhile the Vietnam War was swallowing up more US troops and more helicopters.

The armed Huey lash-ups were no longer enough. Bell had the Iroquois Warrior format and the Sioux Scout test experience to draw on and rapidly put the two together. The dynamics and rotor system of the UH-1C were married to a new front end drawn from the Warrior and Sioux Scout and, by Sept. 1965, the prototype Model 209 'HueyCobra' was made ready for its first flight.

The US Army AAFSS committee were meanwhile anxious to get an interim combat helicopter to southeast Asia. Before them were modified versions of the Sikorsky S-61, the Kaman UH-2, the Piasecki 16H and the big, tandem-rotor Boeing-Vertol CH-47A. The Piasecki and Boeing Vertol were quickly eliminated, although armed ACH-47As were combat-

Above: Bell AH-1T improved TOW-carrying SeaCobra for the US Marine Corps. USMC attack helicopters are embarked aboard US Navy amphibious assault ships.

Below: Key to the AH-64A's all-weather combat ability is the PN Pilot's Night Vision and Target Acquisition and Designation system mounted in the prominent nose turret.

The AH-64A equipped with laser seeking Hellfire missiles will give the US Army a formidable, if highly expensive, all-weather anti-tank armour capability.

evaluated in Vietnam during 1966. The other entries were flown off in tests from Nov. 1965 and, in April the next year, the winner was announced—the Bell 209 HueyCobra, standardized as the AH-1G, with an initial order for 100 machines.

The first HueyCobras arrived in Vietnam in Aug. 1967. As originally outfitted they carried a 7·62-mm six-barrel rotary Minigun in an Emerson Electric TAT-102A rapid-slewing chin turret. This was soon replaced by the XM-28 armament system, with twin 7·62-mm Miniguns or XM-129 40-mm grenade launchers or one of each. Under its stub wings the AH-1G could carry rocket or Minigun pods, but these were relatively inaccurate.

Meanwhile the full AAFSS requirement was still very much alive. The front runner, as the first AH-1Gs were actually entering service in Vietnam, was Lockheed's AH-56 Cheyenne. The AH-56 was extremely ambitious indeed. It attempted to combine the most advanced techniques in helicopter dynamics and construction with equally advanced avionics and armament system, so as to allow operations with a formidable lift of weapons in all weather and at high speed. It was big, weighing over five tons (the HueyCobra weighed a third less) and was a 'compound' helicopter, with a three-bladed pusher propeller and a four-bladed rigid lift rotor. The avionics fit as designed featured terrain-following radar, Doppler radar, inertial navigational systems, an all-weather autopilot, and day and night sensors. Moreover, the whole machine was further weighed down by barbette-mounted cannon and air-launched TOW anti-armour missiles. It was phenomenally expensive and even the US Army could not afford it. The project was finally cancelled in 1969, 18 months, in fact, after the US Army had signed for an initial order of 375 production Cheyennes.

Meanwhile, the 'interim' HueyCobras soldiered on in Vietnam, US Army pilots developing the tactics for the new kind of aircraft and a seemingly insatiable appetite for many more of these machines—838 were on order by Oct. 1968 and a further 240 in 1970-1. This fact also conspired to kill the Lockheed Cheyenne and the success of the AH-1G removed the urgent necessity for an immediate and much more expensive follow-on. Meanwhile, the basic HueyCobra had been developed into a twin-engined over-water model for the US Marine Corps (the AH-1J SeaCobra, first deliveries of which began in 1970) and the AH-1Q equipped with eight TOW anti-tank missiles.

Bell developed a stretched HueyCobra, called the KingCobra, to compete with Sikorsky's S-67 Black-hawk in the last round of the AAFSS contest in 1972, but already the US Army was losing interest. The requirement was reissued in 1973 as the Advanced Attack Helicopter (AAH) specification, the first operational results of which are entering service today as the Hughes AH-64 Apache.

The shift in emphasis was from helicopters as aerial platforms for counter-insurgency to a machine which could fly and fight in the most intensive of all-out wars —in all weathers, in the face of heavy ground fire and against heavily armoured targets. To do this the

The Apache may be the last US combat helicopter built from traditional materials. The ACAP programme is developing airframes constructed entirely of composites.

helicopter has to carry weapons capable of defeating armour at long ranges but at the same time must itself survive. Its prime defence is its agility.

US pilots were using the helicopter's unique aerial slipperiness to develop 'scoot and shoot' tactics as early as the Korean War. In Vietnam these were refined into 'nap of the earth' techniques, which means taking advantage of natural cover including trees, hills or buildings, while 'popping-up' only for a brief reconnaissance or strike. Because helicopters operate in a completely different environment as regards speed and space from fixed-wing aircraft they have a certain immunity to air-to-air interception,

although not of course to guided missiles or to ground fire. The amount of armour lifted by the current generation attack helicopter comes close to justifying the label 'flying tanks'.

The second requirement is for a target acquisition, sighting and weapon system which is light enough to carry aloft but capable of tank killing at long range. The first-generation answer lay in wire-guided, hollow-charge anti-tank missiles, a concept first pioneered in Europe. The French were successful in the early 1950s with the wire-guided SS-10 anti-tank missile, soon supplanted by the bigger SS-11. The air-launched version, or AS-11, was first tested on a French Army Alouette in 1958 and the concept seemed immediately attractive. A missile could be launched from a helicopter in flight, be tracked by the aerial gunner and manually guided to impact by commands sent through trailing wires. This first-generation technique, where the gunner has to keep both missile (aided by a tracking flare) and target in his line of sight, is called MACLOS (Manual Command to Line of Sight) guidance. The helicopter gunner has an advantage not enjoyed by his infantry counterpart —because a helicopter can attack armour from different angles and, effectively, from above he can find the weakest aspect of a tank's plated hide while moving across terrain at high speed, as the tactical situation demands.

The US Army began experimenting with the French AS-11 in 1960 and used it effectively in Vietnam some five years later. The West German

As well as Hellfire anti-tank missiles, the AH-64A can fire up to 76 2·75-in folding fin rockets or engage targets with its 30-mm Chain Gun.

Above: The Hughes-developed XM230E1 Chain Gun is mounted between the main wheel legs and has a rate of fire of 800 rds/minute, with a maximum load of 1200 rounds.

Below: The Hughes Black Hole infrared suppression system uses special ejector nozzles to deflect the hot engine exhaust into the rotor downwash.

Army and the British Army Air Corps were also testing AS-11s in the early 1960s and began to experiment actively in the whole new tactical arena of helicopter versus armour. The AS-11 became standardized in British Army service on the Westland Scout helicopter and this somewhat elderly combination was deployed in the Falklands fighting of 1982, where the missile hit rate was in fact very high.

The Soviet Union was not slow to monitor US and European armed helicopter developments as a weapon for both guerrilla counterinsurgency in southeast Asia and for a NATO war in Europe. Machine guns and rockets were attached to Mi-4 Hounds and Mi-6 Hooks in the 1960s, and the first-generation Soviet wire-guided ATGM, the AT-3 Sagger, was being wired up for helicopter firing soon after its regular infantry appearance in 1965.

As pointed out MACLOS guidance demanded a great deal of a skilled gunner even before he was attempting to engage armour from within a vibrating, jinking helicopter. The second generation of ATGMs employ Semi-Automatic Command to Line of Sight (SACLOS) guidance. This requires only that the target be kept in track, the missile being picked up automatically by an infrared sensor, which tracks its flare and generates signals along the trailing wires to bring it into the gunner's line of sight and thus enable it to impact upon the target. In the late 1960s the

Helicopter Air-to-Air Combat

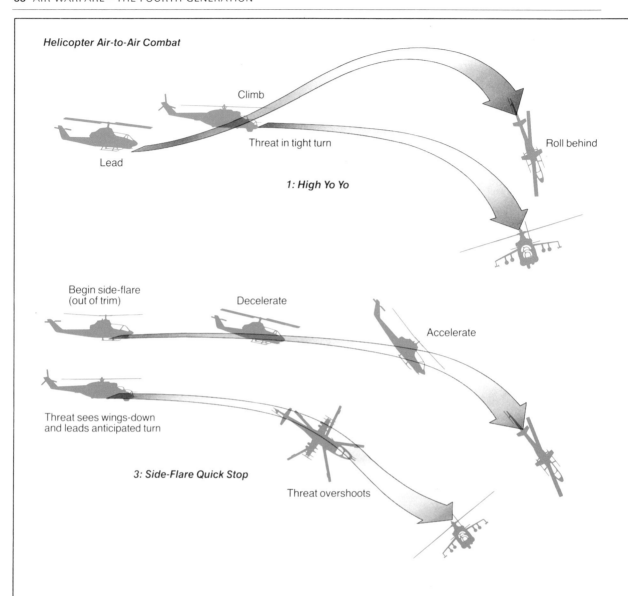

Climb

Threat in tight turn

Lead

Roll behind

1: High Yo Yo

Begin side-flare
(out of trim)

Decelerate

Accelerate

Threat sees wings-down
and leads anticipated turn

3: Side-Flare Quick Stop

Threat overshoots

Helicopter air-to-air combat

While to date any actual helicopter-to-helicopter combat has been a
rarity, many specialists believe that the most formidable foe helicopters
will face in any major conflict of the future would be another helicopter,
perhaps specially designed for the purpose, duelling for air superiority
among the treetops and fighting it out with cannon fire and air-to-air
missiles.

These diagrams show some of the manoeuvres and tactics developed
by US pilots in the last few years, with US Army pilots flying AH-1S
Cobras and US Marine Corps pilots flying bigger CH-53s to simulate
potential threat helicopters such as the Soviet Hind-D.

Figure 1 shows the manoeuvre known as the High Yo Yo. In each case
the Cobra pilot is trying to get on the Hind's tail, just as in fixed-wing
combat, but some manoeuvres employ the helicopter's unique ability to
accelerate or decelerate in mid air, even to stop dead. The High Yo Yo,

however, is a variation on the fixed-wing theme – once the threat aircraft
has shown the direction of his break, then the pursuer climbs, avoids an
overshoot and rolls into the threat's rear. At short range, the pursuer
breaks towards the threat helicopter and forces him to overshoot. At
longer range it is apparently better to lower the helicopter's nose and
start a defensive pull up with a rolling climb which will still cause the threat
to overshoot at lower altitude. Figure 2 shows the horizontal scissors
which is a defensive tactic to throw off a pursuer and come out on his tail.

The defending pilot increases his turn rate until the threat either
overshoots or moves outside his turn radius. As the threat passes, the
direction of turn is reversed and, once behind and below, the pilot strives
to remain in phase with the threat's manoeuvres. To counter this
manoeuvre the advice is not to turn hard or reduce power but to keep up
the airspeed by dropping the rate of turn, then climb and wait for the
threat to cross in front of you. If the threat does not reverse his turn, the

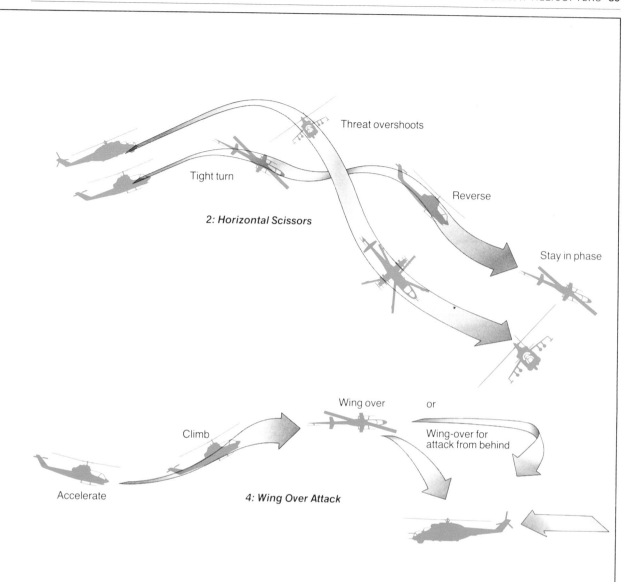

Threat overshoots

Tight turn

2: Horizontal Scissors

Reverse

Stay in phase

Wing over

or

Wing-over for
attack from behind

Climb

Accelerate

4: Wing Over Attack

defender is advised to perform a High Yo Yo and break contact.

The third diagram shows the Side Flare Quick Stop, a manoeuvre developed by US Marine Corps pilots which most exploits the helicopter's special aerial agility. It is designed to cause the threat to overshoot when engaging at ranges below 150 km. The defender rapidly applies contrary controls and reduces power which puts the helicopter out of trim. The threat now sees the target wings down and apparently about to turn but in fact it is rapidly decelerating causing the threat to overshoot. At this stage the defender should accelerate to come out on the threat's tail.

A defence against the side flare is to start a zoom climb to mask your helicopter behind the opponent's own rotor disc while at the same time giving you the height to start a diving attack.

The fourth diagram shows the Wing-Over attack which is an offensive manoeuvre used in head-on engagements or those with only a small

angle-off.

It begins by accelerating towards the target and then making a rapid climb to get the advantage of altitude while the threat's own rotor disc will mask his weapons. Once the right altitude is reached the tactic next involves rolling in towards the threat target and aiming for a point in the dive midway between one's own and the target's position over the ground.

The recommended defence against the Wing Over attack is to climb and turn towards the threat after it has committed itself to its diving attitude. The usual result is the two aircraft going into a turning corkscrew series of manoeuvres as both pilots try to come out above each other's tail.

The latest Soviet combat helicopter, the Mi-28, has been reported as being light and agile, and is smaller than the ground-attack Mi-24 Hind. It has been suggested that it has been especially designed from the outset and is equipped with weapons for the anti-helicopter air-to-air role.

The Boeing-Vertol CH-47 Chinook is the most widely serving heavy-lift helicopter in the world, operational with many air forces. A single RAF Chinook in the Falklands lifted prodigious loads without problems. The US Army has embarked on a modernization programme to bring earlier models up to CH-47D standard.

The standard heavy-lift helicopter of the US Marine Corps is the CH-53 Super Stallion. Around 100 CH-53Ds are in service, with 33 of the more powerful CH-53E on order.

Soviets equipped the Sagger with SACLOS guidance and the hit rate probability rose from 60% to over 90%. At the same time a development of the AT-2 Swatter, with a radio rather than wire command link, appeared. The overall effectiveness of the new generation of Soviet ATGMs was amply demonstrated in the hands of Arab infantry in the 1973 Middle East war.

Western nations did not need the lesson underlined. The Franco-German Euromissile consortium was meanwhile developing the HOT wire-guided ATGM, while the bigger Hughes TOW missile represented the US equivalent. Both used optical tracking with semi-SACLOS guidance and both were subsequently adapted for use from helicopters. HOT is the primary anti-tank missile of the French and German helicopter forces. Work on a helicopter-borne TOW proceeded in parallel with ground launch from the mid-1960s. Two UH-1Bs modified to carry TOW destroyed 24 enemy armoured vehicles in a six-week combat trial in Vietnam during 1972 and later that year a few TOW-carrying HueyCobras were tested in action as AH-1Qs.

With the AH-1G HueyCobra now in service in very large numbers and the US Army no longer committed to large-scale ground war in Vietnam, the new tank-killing technology was engineered into the existing fleet. Half the AH-1G force was earmarked for conversion to TOW-capable AH-1Q standard, while the remainder was re-engineered to AH-1S standard, with optically flat cockpit panels and laser target acquisition systems. The AH-1S carries eight TOWs and a three-barrel 20-mm cannon. Up to 76 folding fin rockets can be mounted in place of the two quad TOW launchers.

In spite of the size and scale of upgrading of the AH-1 force, the US Army never lost its commitment to the dedicated AAFSS concept, albeit in modified form (Advanced Attack Helicopter). In June 1973 design contracts were awarded to Hughes and Bell to build prototypes for competitive testing of the AAH. Three and a half years later, after an intense contest between Bell's YAH-G3 and the Hughes YAH-64, Hughes won and Bell went back to AH-1 production and remanufacture.

From the first prototype flight in 1975 to the AH-64 Apache's initial entry into service with the US Army in Europe will take ten years, itself indicative of the complexity of the system (the AH-1G took two years, admittedly under the pressure of the Vietnam war). The Apache is a combination of highly capable weapons platform, equipped with very sophisticated target acquisition, together with night and adverse weather operations equipment and equally advanced weapons systems, in particular laser-guided Hellfire anti-tank missiles. Sixteen Hellfires with a range of up to 6 km (3·7 mi.) are carried. The Hellfire has been under development by Rockwell International since 1971 and is an all-weather system, a generation ahead of the TOW-type SACLOS missiles. It works by having a laser seeker in its nose (*see* box feature), which uses a development of the infrared homing principle but tuned to the pulsed light codes generated by laser designators. Hellfire is a 'fire and forget' missile, in that its seeker will steer the missile towards a target illuminated by either the Apache's own designator, a ground- or vehicle-based designator or one in another aircraft.

With all these capabilities, however, fire control in the fog of battle becomes more problematic. Remote designation requires an exchange of information between helicopter and the designator about where the target is, whether to lock on before launch and what code to use. When multiple targets and a number of helicopters are involved the problems become even greater, without even considering enemy electronic countermeasures and jamming. The AH-64 Apache, however, is well able to take care of its own fire control, with a system that would have been worthy of a battleship firing 16-inch broadsides. The heart of the system is the so-called TADS/PNV — Target Acquisition and Designation/Pilot's Night Vision. The sensors are mounted in a turret at the extreme nose, which can turn through 120° right and left and +30° or −60° in elevation. It incorporates a direct-view telescope with magnification of ×3·5 and ×6, a vidicon TV, a laser ranger, designator and spot tracker, together with forward-looking infrared which is the primary night vision device. The TV can penetrate daytime haze and, coupled with the direct view optics, the system allows the gunner to identify targets long before the human eye could pick them up. Further, the TV can track

targets automatically by locking on to contrasting borders between, say, a tank and a heathland background.

Gunner and pilot are lavishly provided with displays and automatic systems simply to make possible the daunting task of flying a fast and highly mobile platform so close to the ground while engaging targets at long range at night in sleeting rain. As well as an optical relay tube displaying TADS information, the gunner (who also has flight controls available and acts as co-pilot) has a look-down cathode ray tube display and the IHADSS, the integrated helmet and display sighting system, which projects information into the crew member's line of sight via a monocle attached to the flight helmet. Although it can only be used at night, the IHADSS system gives the crew the ability to take in the mass of information they need to fly the helicopter and operate the weapons, while remaining acutely aware of the real world around them.

During night flying with the PNVS the IHADSS symbology shows the pilot where the fuselage is pointing as he turns his head to scan the countryside over which he is about to fly, while other symbols flash up height, speed and acceleration. The enhanced view through the PNVS will clearly show vegetation against rock, buildings, contours and even, it is claimed, detect high-tension cables. The helmet sight can be used to aim the chain gun or to steer the TADS on to a target detected by the pilot. The pilot can also see on his head-down multi-purpose display the picture seen by the gunner through his optical relay tube.

The system can be switched to a 'pop-up' mode, where the pilot can climb out of a sheltered spot where the Apache is hovering at night, take a look

The Aerospatiale SA 330 Puma is the standard assault helicopter of the French army. Over 40 Westland-built Pumas serve with the RAF. Above is the AS 332 Super Puma.

round, then return to the same spot by following the symbology. Further, the pilot can pop up, allowing the co-pilot to momentarily view the scene ahead with the TADS, which in effect takes a snapshot of what is out there. While back in cover the gunner can view a recording of the frozen TADS picture in order to select targets for a second pop up and immediate Hellfire launch.

An engagement sequence begins when the gunner identifies a target, either with his own eyes or with the direct view optics, while the TV can lock on as soon as the target is identified.

The laser is activated and a missile imparted with the designator's code and set for high- or low-trajectory launch. The missile can be launched with its seeker already locked on to the target or locking on after launch, thus allowing the helicopter to stand off under cover. In order to prevent the laser spot being detected by the target, it can be positioned to one side and swung on to the target just before impact.

The TADS can memorize the position of one target while being used to scan the landscape beyond, and two targets can be lodged in the memory simultaneously. Two missiles following the same laser guidance code can be fired in sequence, with two seconds between them. As soon as the first missile strikes, the gunner moves the laser spot to the second target and the second Hellfire will automatically change course to follow it. In ripple fire two or more separate designators, using different codes preset in the missile's seekers, allow a much faster rate of fire.

Apaches come at a price of $7 million each, even though costs could be spread over a production run of

The Soviet Mi-24 Hind has been described as a low-speed ground-attack aircraft rather than an assault helicopter proper. Its stub wings confer high speed and a good weapons lift but at the expense of manoeuvrability. Nose armament (*below*) is a four-barrel, high-velocity rotary cannon, and the stub wings mount guided anti-tank missiles or unguided rocket pods.

more than 500. That price does not include the considerable extra cost of special training and ground equipment (estimated at $3 million per unit) or the US Army's massive $1300 million research and development bill. At these prices, a way of making existing fleets of attack helicopters night- and bad-weather capable becomes very attractive.

The Cobra AH-1S uses the M65 daylight telescopic sight unit mounted in the nose, with $\times 3 \cdot 2$ and $\times 13$ magnification capability. The British Army Lynx has a similar sight mounted in the roof, and the French Army Gazelle and German Bo 105P also have their SFIM 397 sights positioned in the less vulnerable roof position.

The best solution of all would be a sight mounted above the rotor (a 'mast-mounted sight' or MMS), but considerable engineering problems of stress and vibration have to be overcome. A modified mast-mounted M65 sight has been flown in a small Hughes 500MD, TOW missiles have been launched

successfully in tests, and a French Ophelia sight has been test-flown in a MMS installation on a Bo 105CB. McDonnell Douglas is the primary contractor for a mast-mounted sight for the US Army's Army Helicopter Improvement Programme (AHIP), designed to give enhanced combat capability to the large fleet of OH-58 Kiowa Scout helicopters.

European NATO anti-tank helicopters do not currently have the ability to fight at night unless targets are illuminated by flares. While it would be relatively easy to build in passive infrared gunner's sights, they are relatively expensive and bulky and it is probable that effective night vision goggles will be the answer to the short-term upgrading of capabilities. Night vision goggles intensify ambient light, such as starlight or moonlight, but by no means are they the ideal answer.

The design emphasis of Western attack helicopters has been all about survival through low-level agility, even at the expense of speed. Faced with ever thickening ground fire in the Vietnam war, however, and especially with the new threat of the SA-7 Grail infantry-fired, heat-seeking missile, the US Cobra pilots adopted high-speed diving tactics, leaving as little time over the target as possible. Soviet attack helicopters are very different from their Western counterparts but, ironically, they are tuned to the basically fixed-wing tactics employed by American attack helicopter pilots in Vietnam. The Mi-24 Hind, looked at in detail below, is the primary Soviet attack

The Hind-D's prominent nose probe is thought to be a slow airspeed sensing device, while the under-nose sensor pack could include radar and low-light level TV, plus, possibly, forward-looking infrared.

helicopter and is designed to use not terrain but rather speed and heavy armour as the means to survival. The latest Hind-E model has in fact been described as a low-speed, low-level ground-attack fighter rather than an assault helicopter.

As already outlined, the first Soviet experiments with armed helicopters began in the late 1960s. Around 1967 the Mil design bureau was given the task of developing a kind of hybrid, an armed helicopter which retained the capacity to land a squad of eight troops in the heart of the battle. The Hind-A model began production in early 1973, preceded by an experimental version (Hind-B) without wingtip-guided weapon rails and without the pronounced anhedral (downward canting) of the stub wings. The Hind's wings illustrate the Soviet designers' approach. At high speed they offload the rotor providing 25% of the lift, but in the hover they interfere with the rotor downwash, degrading performance and low-speed manoeuvrability—which is the essence of Western combat helicopter design. The Hind is also optimized for high-speed flight in having that rarity among helicopter features, a retractable undercarriage.

The first Hind-As entered service with Soviet Frontal Aviation in East Germany in 1974. In service the Hind A apparently exceeded expectations and so it

The US Army's huge LHX advanced helicopter requirement has prompted US manufacturers to produce many concepts, including this light utility scout attack proposal by Sikorsky.

was decided to develop it into a much more formidable attack helicopter, with all-weather and anti-armour capability. The rear fuselage main rotor and transmission are common to all Hind models, but the Hind D featured a completely new forward fuselage arranged with stepped gunner's and pilot's cockpit in HueyCobra manner, while a flight engineer is accommodated in the cabin. The Hind D is extensively armoured along its undersurface and around the crew positions, and key dynamic components are similarly protected.

The Hind D mounts a large turret beneath the nose, containing a four-barrel rotary 12·7-mm gun, a high-velocity, high-rate-of-fire weapon, with an estimated range of 1500 m, which can function in ground attack or in the air-to-air role, engaging enemy helicopters. The gun is stabilized and can be directed at will by the gunner or fired fixed forward by the pilot.

The Hind Models A-D and the latest E-model (basically a Hind D with more sophisticated avionics) can carry a heavy load of weapons, up to one ton on each stub wing. A typical load consists of four rocket pods, each holding up to 32 unguided anti-armour rockets with a range of 1200 m. Four guided anti-tank missiles can be accommodated on the two wingtips—on the Hind A and D these are usually AT-2 Swatter Bs with a range of up to four km. The Hind E model carries four AT-9 Spiral missiles, with a range of up to five km and an armour-penetrating power 50% greater than that of the Swatter.

Both AT-2 and AT-6 are SACLOS-guided—all the gunner has to do is keep the target in his crosshair—but they differ from the equivalent western TOW and HOT missiles in possessing radio-command guidance rather than having to pass aiming information down trailing wires to the missile in flight. Radio guidance is more technically compact and tactically more easily handled but is vulnerable to electronic counter-measures.

Helicopter-to-helicopter combat
Just as tanks were for years regarded as the most effective weapon against other tanks, so many armies, considering the best way to counter the attack helicopter, see a future in dedicated anti-helicopter helicopters battling for air superiority amongst the treetops. There have been persistent reports of a specialized air-to-air helicopter, the Mi-28, being developed in the Soviet Union, while NATO armies have drafted specifications for a counterpart.

The current line-up of first division anti-tank helicopters are not ideally suited to aerial combat. The Hind D and E are large, heavy and fast and could outrun the US Cobra and AH-64 Apache but would be outmanoeuvred in low-speed combat, where the primary weapons would be a stabilized multi-barrel cannon. The current fit of unguided ground-attack rockets or wire- and laser-guided anti-tank missiles, with fire control systems optimized for anti-armour attack, makes scoring a hit with gun or missile on a rapidly manoeuvring target seem highly problematic. Specialized helicopter AAMs are under development and include modifications of fixed-wing AAMs, such as AIM-9 Sidewinders already mounted on US Marine Corps AH-1s and tested on the AH-64, and small SAMs, such as the US Stinger and British Blowpipe, which are both being evaluated in the anti-helicopter role. A helicopter version of the Matra SATCP AAM, called Mistral, is planned. This is a 'fire-and-forget'

infrared-seeking missile which accelerates very quickly, reaching a distance of 4000 m in under six second. The US Vought Company and British Aerospace have an agreement to develop a guided air-to-air hyper-velocity missile, which is even faster—travelling 4000 m in 3·5 seconds.

The US Army has an extensive programme, called Ahip (attack helicopter improvement programme), to rework its large fleet of OH-58A Kiowa scout helicopters to C and D standard, including fitting a proportion with air-to-air missiles, probably a version of the Stinger SAM. The US Army is not going to arm AH-64s with air-to-air missiles but is keeping them dedicated to their primary anti-armour role.

Beyond Ahip is the US Army's huge LHX requirement for no fewer than 6000 advanced combat helicopters to replace AH-1s, OH-6s and OH-58s (LHX-SCAT) and UH-1s (LHX-U). The programme is based on the Airland-Battle 2000 premise and is very much concerned with air-to-air combat right from the outset. The US Army expects airfields for fixed-wing aircraft to be obliterated in the opening stages of any European war and thus has an ambitious requirement for a multirole helicopter, capable of autonomous operation from dispersed sites in all weathers, over any terrain and round the clock. Not only should such machines survive in aerial combat but they should be able to make attacks on second-echelon targets deep inside enemy territory. The Army plans to meet this requirement with a streamlined front line of AH-64As, LHX and troop-carrying UH-60s.

The LHX technology programme comes under the banner title, advanced rotorcraft technology integration (ARTI), which is pushing the concept to the limits as much as any fixed-wing counterpart. Integrated digital avionics and the fruits of the VHSIC pro-gramme will yield immensely capable computing power and even on-board artificial intelligence. Combine this with the 'sensor fusion' concept and the human task of flying and fighting at night a few feet from the ground at 160 knots begins to look possible. Sensor fusion will integrate information from advanced sensors, such as millimetre wave imaging radar, FLIR and carbon dioxide laser radars, and present it in coherent form with threats and tasks shown in order of priority. Digital flight controls will be used, with signals transmitted through the airframe by fibre optics. The speed requirement has not been set. If it is below 300 knots then an advancing blade rotor will be used; if higher speeds are required then tilt rotors will probably be employed.

European manufacturers are staying in the advanced combat helicopter business in spite of the expense. The Agusta A.129 prototype anti-tank helicopter first flew in late 1983 and is on order for the Italian army. The British Army Air Corps wants 250 all-weather/night-capable combat helicopters by the late 1980s, perhaps divided between air-to-air and air-to-ground dedicated types, and is looking at a new and enlarged version of the Lynx. The Franco-German PAH-2 programme has not been trouble-free, with France wanting an air-to-air-capable version, first to protect its existing fleet of anti-tank Gazelles armed with HOT missiles. In addition, Britain, France and West Germany will all require a new transport helicopter in the late 1980s to replace Pumas and UH-1s, and a new light helicopter family is another prize for industry.

CHAPTER 4

Electronic Warfare Aircraft

Modern weapon systems depend for their effectiveness on being able to bring devastating force together in time and place—at high speed, at long range, in all weathers and with scant regard for human error.

The electronic battlefield, whether on land, sea or in the air, depends on a finely tuned network of electronic command and control. The weapon systems it brings into action themselves depend on electronics for their individual concentrations of destructive power. The electromagnetic spectrum, therefore, has become as important an arena for war as any more visibly contested terrain.

During World War II the existence of radar and electronic navigation equipment was crucial to the outcome of major campaigns of the air war, from the Battle of Britain to the strategic bombing of Germany, although electronics made little impact on the mass tactical air warfare of the eastern front. Today, in the Soviet Union just as much as in the west, electronic warfare (EW) is a very important military consideration, touching every aspect of air power. Modern combat aircraft will show a combination of the following EW capabilities, depending on their role and degree of technical sophistication: electronic counter-measures and electronic counter-countermeasures; target acquisition, target tracking, display and designation; navigation—stellar, doppler, radio, inertial, radar, terrain-following; weapons management, fibre-optic flight controls, power supply, servo-control, fault-diagnosis, communications and so on.

Electronics represent today a third of the USAF's equipment costs and the proportion of research funding it commands is more than that for weapons, airframes or propulsion. USAF Systems Command looks after over 40,000 computers and 250,000 further individual black boxes within its fleets of aircraft. The pressures this puts on a modern air force are threefold. The first is recruiting, training and keeping highly skilled technical manpower. Maintaining the serviceability of these flying computers is the second vitally important factor. There is little point in displaying a reassuring list of available aircraft if one by one they are going to become unserviceable, owing to a defective electronic component, with spares warehoused thousands of miles from the scene of action. Cost is the third factor because the acceleration in the application of electronics, far from making weapon systems cheaper, has served to push up the price from one generation to another, at a pace far greater than that of general inflation.

The reward for this vast expense is survival. Without constant research and development and the ability to quickly apply the results to the practical battlefield situation, the manned combat aircraft becomes expensively and embarrassingly vulnerable. The Middle East War of Oct. 1973 made the importance of EW very clear—an integrated and modern air defence missile system shielded Egyptian

The Grumman E-2C Hawkeye is the standard early-warning aircraft of the US Navy, but has shown its electronic force-multiplying abilities in Israeli service.

aircraft from attack at their bases, in contrast to the experience of 1967 when they were destroyed in droves on the ground. Israeli pilots felt the effects of communications jamming even as they sat in their cockpits before takeoff. In the first six days of the 18-day war almost 100 Israeli aircraft were destroyed by SA-6 surface-to-air missiles guided by continuous wave radars, while ZSU-23 radar-guided multiple cannon and man-portable heat-seeking SA-7s made low-level attack equally dangerous. In Israel's June 1982 invasion of the Lebanon the contrast could not have been more complete. Aircraft losses were nil, the Syrian SAM defences being neutralized by a brilliantly efficient electronic countermeasures offensive.

Expendable unmanned IAI Scout drones were sent over the enemy SA-6 batteries in the Bekkaa valley to draw their fire, while their electronic signatures were registered by Grumman E2-C Hawkeye EW aircraft. The recorded electronic intelligence (Elint) was programmed into aircraft jammers, which were then able to blanket air defence frequencies and make the missiles effectively inoperable. Large numbers of decoy gliders were also launched by F-4s to saturate Syrian SAM sites. Such systems as the Brunswick Maxi-decoy used by the Israeli air force can dispense chaff as they glide along at high speed, drop flares, or carry jammers or radar signature augmentation to give them the appearance of a real aircraft. The US Navy stormed into the Lebanon in late 1983 and very quickly lost carrier aircraft (an A-7E and an A-6E) to Syrian SA-9 heat-seeking missiles, drawing Israeli scorn for their lack of sophistication in tactics (flying too low and too slowly) if not for their extensive fit of electronic warfare equipment.

Electronic intelligence (Elint)

Elint is defined as 'electronic intelligence gathering—the activity of monitoring, measuring, identifying and analysing hostile electromagnetic radiation of any kind, across the electromagnetic spectrum from DC to light.'

Anything which is 'active' in the sense of emitting detectable radiation will automatically signal more than just its own presence—it gives away the location

Ilyushin Il-38 May anti-submarine warfare aircraft. Some ten basically similar Il-10 Coots serve as electronic intelligence-gathering platforms with Soviet Naval Aviation.

Beechcraft U-21F of the US Army. Modified as RU-21Js, three of these aircraft serve as sensor platforms for the US Army's Cefly Lancer programme.

of its carrier and possibly its speed, course and height.

Furthermore, the characteristics of the emission act as a fingerprint—the basic frequency, the pulse repetition frequency, the amplitude (that is, the height of each pulse above the baseline), the time of arrival and direction—all will give away vital clues as to just what is out there. The new generation of modern combat aircraft, therefore, are equipped with an array of radar warning receivers (RWR), which passively pick up the hostile emissions, and computers to analyse the results. The RWR will identify the nature of the threat by comparing the hostile emitter's 'signature' with electronic models stored in a 'threat library'. These models will have been made from inputs collected on special Elint gathering missions (*see* below). If a hostile tracking radar has achieved lock-on it will make itself known as a high frequency pulse sustained for a quantifiable period of time (up to several seconds). Audible and visual alarms will make the crew aware of what is happening, and the system should sort out and identify the most immediately dangerous threat and provide a link-up with the next step—the operation of the aircraft's own electronic countermeasures.

The USAFs F-15 Eagle was designed from the outset with an internal tactical electronic warfare system (TEWS), which consists of the Loral-developed AN/ALR-56 radar warning receiver system and the Northrop ALQ-135 active jammer. The RWR consists of four circularly polarized spiral antennae, each within its own small radome, facing forward on the wing and aft on the fin tips and providing 360° coverage of high frequency signals. A blade antenna beneath the forward fuselage watches below for low-band emitters. Intercepted signals are fed into a pre-processor and general-purpose digital computer within the airframe, both pre-programed with information gleaned from previous Elint operations about the expected 'threat environment'. As the vital intelligence is processed, it is relayed to the pilot on his countermeasures display—with evaluations of the threat, its bearing and distance—in clear, high-contrast symbols, readable in bright sunlight so that rapid defensive manoeuvres can be effected.

The active jamming component of the F-15's tactical electronic warfare system uses a travelling wave tube (TWT) to generate the large amount of microwave energy required to blanket an incoming hostile signal, while the computer, guided by inputs from the radar warning receiver system, is all the time striving to assign priority to changing threats and to direct the most appropriate response.

The problem is that the hostile emitter may well be a surface-to-air or air-to-air missile closing at supersonic speed, employing its own active radar terminal or semi-active radar mid-course guidance and equipped with its own electronic counter-countermeasures, while hopping from one frequency to another thousands of times a second. Sheer brute force is one solution—pumping out power in all directions over the entire spread of frequencies at which the threat might operate, but this requires a large input of power and strenuous efforts to keep everything cool. At high speed a ram air-driven turbine can provide the power and bypass cooling, but liquid cooling has advantages for certain applications within the airframe.

Windmill turbogenerators to provide the power and cooling are more effective in 'pod' applications, mounted beneath the airframe and, although they take up a proportion of the useful load which otherwise might be dedicated to weapons, pod mounting permits flexibility in maintenance and operational readiness, and allows older airframes to be rapidly retrofitted to survive in the face of new threats. The USAF's ALQ-131 advanced ECM pod, for example, developed by Westinghouse and now in production by them, is compatible with the older F-4, F-111 and A-7 aircraft, together with the 1970s-generation F-15, F-16 and A-10, and comes in various structural configurations to fit particular aircraft. The system can operate in the blanket jamming 'noise' mode or in the so-called 'deception' mode (*see* below), and has a computerized integral receiver-processor which analyses hostile signals and directs ECM operation against them, with optimum timing and with as much concentration on the hostile emitter's bandwidths as possible. The 'power

The USAF's EF-111A has been expressly developed as an electronic warfare aircraft with massive jamming power. The tail fin mounted unit (*lower picture*) contains a powerful set of radar and infrared emission warning receivers.

management' concept cuts down on the large amount of energy wasted in crude, broad bandwidth jamming and strives to survive with a rapier rather than a bludgeon for defence.

Deception jamming shows off the elegance of the electromagnetic duel. A hostile radar will 'paint' the target in energy and the processed return signals will provide the information for target acquisition and weapon guidance. These signals, however, do not just reveal the presence of the enemy and a lot about him besides, but they can also be bent and distorted. A transponder (transmitter-responder) in an ECM suite can be programmed to operate each time it receives a pulse of energy from a hostile radar. The pulses which the transponder returns may be smaller, larger or out of synchronicity with the incoming pulses, so the hostile missile or radar-guided gunfire will be left hunting for a phantom target.

A radar-guided missile works by steering itself, according to computer-generated commands, towards what its own radar or the radar of its launch aircraft is seeing. But in spite of sophisticated, miniaturized electronics, neither, as yet, can 'see' in the human sense. Thus, as an alternative to degrading the accuracy of the radar through jamming, it can be presented with a dummy target in the form of a decoy glider or 'chaff'—a cloud of metallic foil which will seem much denser and more metallic and thus a more tempting target than the fleeing aircraft. For maximum effectiveness chaff is made of small strips of film, metallized on the surface with zinc or aluminium, and should, ideally, have a length equal to the wavelength of the hostile emitter.

Acting as a miniature dipole (double-ended rod) aerial efficiently reflecting the hostile radiation, the chaff has to be placed in position as rapidly as possible, shaped so as to form a radar cross-section bigger than the target aircraft. Thus, in most applications it is fired in a small cartridge to burst and bloom into a cloud in under two seconds.

A different technique is used by the Lundy ALE-43 chaff-cutter pod which, instead of punching out a cloud of rapid-bloom chaff pre-cut to various random dipole lengths, will automatically strew into the airstream chaff cut precisely to the length of the hostile emitter's wavelength. Continuous reels of chaff material called 'roving' are fed into a system of rollers, with a cutter yielding a specific combination of dipole lengths. Ram air leading from the nose cone and through the centre section exits at the tail and can punch out a cloud of cut-chaff very quickly.

A more typical lightweight chaff dispenser is the Lundy ALE-29A countermeasures system used on various US Navy tactical aircraft. As well as chaff cartridges it can also fire expendable jammers and infrared flares. Just as a chaff acts as a matador's cape to draw off a radar-guided threat, a flare provides a momentarily more attractive source of heat to draw on the seeker of an infrared guided missile, such as a ground-launched SA-7 or an air-to-air weapon like the Sidewinder. A flare will radiate for about three seconds with an output of 15 km, burning mag-

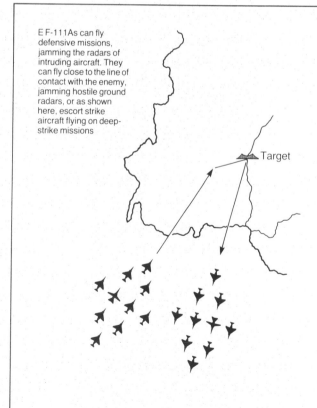

EF-111As can fly defensive missions, jamming the radars of intruding aircraft. They can fly close to the line of contact with the enemy, jamming hostile ground radars, or as shown here, escort strike aircraft flying on deep-strike missions

Target

nesium and tetrafluoroethylene at very high temperature.

Large helicopters of the US Air Force and US Navy use on-board electrical power to create a heat source in a ceramic element which can then be modulated mechanically to produce an infrared jamming signal. Low-speed, low-power aircraft such as the OV-10 are equipped with the Hot Brick System, which burns JP fuel with ram air to heat the ceramic element.

Jammers are the third variety of expandable and they act by degrading the effectiveness of a hostile transmitter or by presenting a phantom target in a burst of high power for a period typically less than 30 seconds. The US ALQ-134 expandable jammer is packed into a mere three cubic inches and is powered by a lithium battery. On ejection, a spring-loaded antenna unfurls and the device begins its descent on a drogue parachute plus parawing, beaming out its deceptive signals.

An aircraft can be detected and targeted by its radar return and by its heat emissions—it can also of course be seen. TV-enhanced target identification systems are used in air superiority aircraft and TV tracking is a component of several important surface-to-air missile systems. Simple smokescreen dispensers have been developed for low-speed aircraft such as helicopters, and specialized electronic warfare aircraft are being developed to act as seeders of smoke and chaff screens in which strike aircraft might operate.

USAF's Aeronautical Systems Division is developing a somewhat less passive countermeasure against the optically guided threat, with the operator as the target. The 'advanced optical countermeasures pod' system will detect the flashes of anti-aircraft gunfire, then use a low-power laser to calculate the range. Finally, a high-power laser is directed at the aiming point to blind the operators or burn out the optical sighting mechanism. Development is planned for use with US tactical aircraft, while the USAF wants it for both air-to-air and air-to-ground defence of B-52 bombers.

One of the reasons why the USAF's B-52 force has remained operational for so long is that the big airframe has been able to absorb engineering changes and new equipment to keep it up to date electronically, since the missile threat it faces today bears no relation to that which it faced when it first flew. Other large airframes of similar vintage have been consistently adapted as dedicated platforms for electronic intelligence gathering and airborne early warning, with no other offensive or defensive functions, whereas another important category of combat aircraft has evolved, separately designed to actively attack the ground-based electronic systems which direct surface-to-air gun and missile defences.

Such early-warning and control aircraft as the Boeing E-3A Sentry and BAe Nimrod Mk 3 fall into

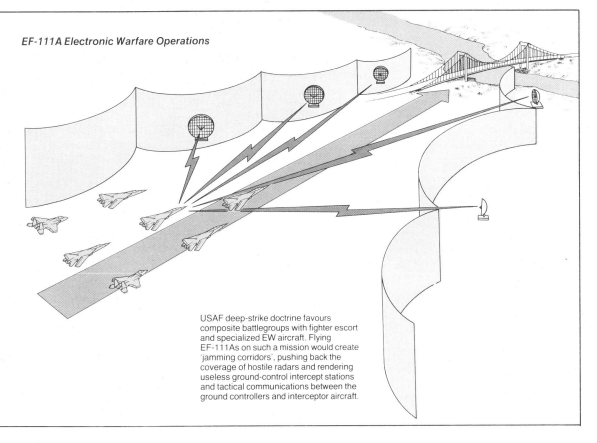

EF-111A Electronic Warfare Operations

USAF deep-strike doctrine favours composite battlegroups with fighter escort and specialized EW aircraft. Flying EF-111As on such a mission would create 'jamming corridors', pushing back the coverage of hostile radars and rendering useless ground-control intercept stations and tactical communications between the ground controllers and interceptor aircraft.

The EA-6B Prowler is the US Navy's dedicated EW aircraft and has been consistently updated in its electronic capabilities. It has a four-man crew.

the first category—unarmed and slow (and both with airframes based on civilian airliners of the 1950s). However, each acts as a force multiplier, able to make air defence far more effective, detecting intruders at long range, over land and over water, and directing their interception with the most efficient application of resources.

Other aircraft of similar breed perform the constant peacetime Elint mission, snooping at the fringes of each other's military activity to record and analyse the constantly shuffling pack of electronic cards. Soviet Il-18 Coot-As shadow NATO naval man-oeuvres in the Atlantic and North Sea, calibrating radar frequencies and listening to tactical C^3 traffic. Big Soviet Bear-Cs, flying out of Murmansk and Cuba, regularly probe UK and US air defences, while US Navy EP-3 Orions and RAF Nimrod R1s graze in the electronic pastures on the Soviet Union's territorial periphery.

The published explanation for the destruction of the Korean Boeing 747 civilian airliner over Soviet territory is that it was assumed to be a US aircraft on an Elint mission. A US RC-135 (similar in configura-tion to the Boeing 707 airliner but based on the KC-135 tanker) was airborne but hundreds of miles

away at roughly the same time. Nevertheless, the failure to distinguish between two very different airframes should shame any professional pilot. The fact remains that USAF RC-135s have performed Elint missions on the border areas of the Soviet Union for more than 20 years, equipped with various systems to collect data on radar performance, to monitor Soviet strategic missile tests, to listen to and relay signals traffic (SIGINT) and, latterly, to gather 'radiation intelligence' (RINT), which monitors radiation from such sources as power lines and motor vehicles.

The USAF's small force of RC-135s in five sub-types are operated by the Strategic Air Command's 55th Strategic Reconnaissance Wing at Offut AFB, Ne-braska, and deployed globally as required. The Israeli air force operates at least one Boeing 707 ex-airliner adapted for Elint missions. Other known Elint platforms in addition to those mentioned above are the Soviet Tupolev Tu-16 Badger and Autonor Cub B, the Israeli Arava light transport, the RAF's Canberra B2, the German Navy's Bréguet Atlantique, French Air Force DC-8s, and the US Army's Sikorsky EH-6 helicopters, Grumman RV-1 Mohawk and Beechcraft RU-21 light transport used for SIGINT (monitoring enemy signal traffic) duties and also operated by Israel.

Such dedicated electronic intelligence aircraft are expected to work at the opposition's border areas in peacetime and not perform penetration missions under fire. Unmanned drones and remotely piloted vehicles have long been studied as platforms for the Elint and optical reconnaissance missions, but the results have been only partially successful. During the Vietnam war more than 3400 sorties were flown by US drones on such missions, with a loss rate of 10%. At the same time ambitious specifications were drafted for very high-flying long-endurance drones for strategic reconnaissance over Soviet and Chinese territory, although satellites were ultimately to fulfil this mission.

After the Vietnam war, research money was absorbed by the new generation of US manned aircraft, and the last remotely piloted vehicle (RPV) squadron in the USAF was stood down in 1978, although drone aerial targets continued to be used extensively.

The Canadair CL-89 Midge surveillance drone is in service with the British, West German, Italian and French armies. It is used for optical and infrared reconnaissance, flying a pre-programmed flightpath and then being recovered by parachute with its recorded information on board. In contrast, the Israeli Scout and large Mastiff RPVs can relay information in 'real time', allowing ground controllers to watch a daylight TV picture of the terrain over which the RPV is flying and even zoom on to and track selected targets. The Mastiff can carry a range of electronic warfare equipment, including jammers and missile decoys, and act as an anti-radiation missile itself, steering towards and destroying a hostile radar.

As well as being used for passive reconnaissance, RPVs are being developed as platforms for the new target acquisition and designation systems which are set to transform the face of conventional warfare. They can carry the laser designation for air- and ground-launched precision-guided munitions and target data for unguided systems such as the Multiple Launch Rocket system (MLRS). Both the US Aquila and British Phoenix RPV projects are specifically required to act as target information for the MLRS.

The use of RPVs as 'harassment drones' for direct attacks on hostile radars is another important avenue of development and brings us back to the offensive component of electronic warfare. The United States and West Germany have been jointly developing the Locust programme for a small winged drone that is pre-programmed to navigate to, and loiter in, an area of hostile air defences. Its presence will either draw fire or cause the radar to shut down. If ignored, it will home in on an emitting radar and destroy it.

Systems such as Locust, the USAF's ground-launched Pave Tiger and the Israeli Mastiff are active defence-suppression weapons. They are also un-manned, cheap and expendable alternatives to a highly exotic and very expensive breed of combat aircraft, whose function is actively to attack enemy radar and ground defence or to lead task forces of strike aircraft into action, providing high-powered electronic countermeasure cover.

When, with Soviet assistance, the North Vietnamese rapidly expanded their surface-to-ground missile capacity in 1965-7, the USAF responded by adapting some old F-100 fighter-bombers as specialized SAM-suppressors, equipped from 1966 onwards with the new AGM-45 Shrike anti-radiation missile. The US Navy began developing the Shrike in the early 1960s primarily as an anti-shipping missile which would home in on the large amount of electromagnetic energy that a warship might emit. The first F-100 'Wild Weasel' (as the defence suppression role was codenamed) made a successful attack on a SA-2 radar in April 1966, but the type could not match the performance of the F-105 Thunderchief ground-attack aircraft it was attempting to escort. Soon the F-105 was adapted to the Wild Weasel role itself, carrying high-power jamming pods and anti-radiation missiles, including the bigger AGM-78 Standard ARM.

By the end of the Vietnam war the defence suppression concept was proved an essential component of air combat, while the need for an even more effective aircraft was apparent. The F-4 Phantom filled the bill and the first Phantom Wild Weasels were converted from F-4C airframes just in time to see some action in the closing stages of the Vietnam war. The F-4G Wild Weasel IIs currently serving the Tactical Air Command were converted from F-4E airframes in the late 1970s and are fitted with the Loral developed AN/APR 38 control indicator set. The system deploys no fewer than 52 special antennae around the airframe, of which the most obvious are in a large pod under the nose and at the top of the vertical tail surface. When it detects a threat it provides the crew with a display—an 'A' symbol representing gunfire control equipment and a number '2', '3' and so on indicating SAM radars types.

Besides classifying the threat the system will rate its potential danger out of a total possible score of 15 and show its range and bearing. In addition, a bomb-aiming system will put the emission source in the centre of the sight's reticle. The offensive weapons load normally consists of three electro-optically guided Maverick missiles on each inner wing pylon, with a Shrike on each outer pylon. The big Standard ARM can be carried, or the new AGM-88 HARM or various other precision-guided air-to-surface weapons. A Westinghouse ALQ-119 jamming pod is mounted conformally in the left-front under-fuselage missile recess, the other three recesses retaining Sparrow air-to-air missiles for self-defence.

The Texas Instruments HARM (High-Speed Anti Radiation Missile) is to replace Shrike and Standard on US Air Force and US Navy aircraft and shows off the new digital technology to advantage. Whereas Shrike had to have a range of homing heads physically changed before a mission, according to the type of emitter expected to be encountered, HARM's on-board computer enables the missile to engage any ship or land-based air defence radar, continuous wave radars, early-warning radars, weather radars, air traffic control radars and so on.

As well as arming dedicated defence suppression aircraft, HARM can provide a self-protection system for any tactical aircraft fitted with radar warning receivers. If a hostile SAM radar should be detected, the HARM computer will analyse the most direct threat and send the missile accelerating at very high speed towards it. The prefragmented 66-kg high-explosive warhead has a laser fuse that senses height above the target and when to detonate for maximum effect.

Such self-protection anti-radiation missiles are now priority systems for air forces dependent on manned, penetrating aircraft. Loading up a HARM or the British Aerospace Alarm (Air-launched anti-radiation missile, on order for the RAF's ground-attack Tornados) may cut a proportion of the useful weapons load, but it gives the manned penetrating aircraft a chance against the tightening mesh of ground-based missile air defence. Even if only a single radar can be destroyed, knowing your radar emissions may be attracting a missile travelling down them at hypersonic speed may cause SAM battery commanders to switch off their radars and thus break the lock. The USAF is working, meanwhile, on a lightweight, self-protection, anti-radiation missile called Sidearm. A Soviet ARM (typenamed AS-9) has been reported, with a range of up to 80 km, arming Su-24 Fencer strike aircraft.

In the Falklands fighting Vulcan bombers of the RAF mounted anti-radiation defence suppression attacks at extreme range and the experience amply illustrates that, in spite of all the wizardry, electronic warfare still has its uncertainties. Once the islands were captured in the initial invasion, Argentinian long-range air surveillance depended on a Westinghouse TPS-43 radar mounted on high ground above Port Stanley. Attacks by Harriers and the first two attacks by Vulcans using iron bombs failed to put the Port Stanley airstrip fully out of action. One of the big bombers was then modified at Ascension Island to carry four AGM-45 Shrikes, with the radar rather than the runway as the target. The Vulcans had already been modified at their Waddington base to carry the Westinghouse AN/ALQ-101D jammer pod (the 'Dash-Ten' pods as the RAF calls them), borrowed from Buccaneers.

In spite of their age the jamming pods apparently confounded the Argentinian surveillance radars and the two Vulcans, which made six separate raids, were unscathed. The first anti-radar mission (Black Buck 4, Vulcan XM 597) was aborted when a Victor tanker became unserviceable. On the second mission (Black Buck XM 597 30/31st May) the Dash-Ten ECM pod was omitted in favour of extra fuel. While Harriers made a strike against Port Stanley, the Vulcan circled, attempting to acquire radar targets but, after three-quarters of an hour and three ineffective missile launches, the bomber turned for home.

Two nights later XM 597 returned. At a range of about 40 km the Vulcan pulled up to expose itself to the main air defence radar, which promptly turned itself off. Again the bomber had to loiter in the area trying to tempt an emitter to switch on, but a partial lock-on only was achieved. The aircraft then turned south to lob missiles ballistically at the target in an attempt to entice a transmission. When one was registered, several missiles were launched and a Shrike reportedly impacted some 80 yards (73 m) off the target, blowing the antenna over but not putting it out of action for more than a few hours. On the return leg the last Shrike remained hung up underneath the aircraft and, during inflight refuelling, the

Above left: A US Navy proposal for new TACAMO strategic missile submarine communications aircraft based on the E-3 airframe has had its budget cut back and looks unlikely, for the time being, to go beyond this artist's impression.
Left: Meanwhile, E-3A Sentries provide the USAF with highly capable airborne detection and control systems.

NATO's E-3A AWACS force is registered to the otherwise non-existent Luxembourg air force. Eighteen Sentries will eventually mount the electronic watch on European NATO's airspace.

probe broke away. The Vulcan had to force-land at Rio de Janeiro with its highly sensitive US-supplied missile dangling beneath. The Shrike was promptly impounded, while XM 597 flew home.

The Black Buck raids gave the RAF live experience in defence suppression, using a rapidly improvised combination of long-range strategic bombers and US tactical jammers and missiles. The RAF has long made clear its requirement for a self-protection anti-radar missile for the Tornado strike aircraft. When the choice had to be made in 1983, the service actually preferred the US HARM, which it would bring into operational service in the mid-1980s. The government went for Alarm, the UK-developed rival, which would enter service a few years later. Meanwhile, observers of British defence policy expect to see proposals for a home-grown RAF 'Wild Weasel' using the Buccaneer or possibly Tornado itself. The West German Naval air arm has plans to provide its Tornados with HARMs and MBB is working on an electronic combat and reconnaissance variant (ECR) which might be equipped with the EF-111A's ALQ-99 jammer.

Meanwhile, the USAF has in Europe something else up its sleeve—the Grumman (General Dynamics) EF-111A, the so-called 'Electric Fox'—which, instead of missiles, uses sheer electronic power and sophistication to blind hostile radars. In fact the US Navy developed such an aircraft first—the Grumman EA-6A electronic warfare aircraft, which evolved from the original Grumman A-6 Intruder carrier strike aircraft of the late 1950s. The first EW sub-type,

NATO's E-3A AWACS force is registered to the otherwise non-existent Luxembourg air force. Eighteen Sentries will eventually mount the electronic watch on European NATO's airspace.

named the A-6B, appeared in response to the need for a dedicated defence suppression aircraft and was used during the Vietnam war, firing Shrikes and Standard ARMs at SAM sites. Later the much more specialized EA-6A appeared, with a bulbous fairing on the fin containing an ALQ-86 surveillance system, and jamming pods and chaff dispensers under the wing.

The A-6B and EA-6A were conversions of existing A-6 airframes but in 1968 an entirely new aircraft first flew—the Grumman EA-6B Prowler with a redesigned forward fuselage accommodating a crew of four, a pilot and three electronic warfare specialists. The heart of the Prowler is the AN/ALQ-99 tactical jamming system (TJS), generating jamming signals aimed against early-warning, ground control intercept, surface-to-air missiles, air intercept and naval radars, with a central computer analysing threat inputs and directing jamming operations. The large amount of power needed comes from turbogenerators on the five underwing equipment pods, each containing two very high-powered jammers and a tracker/receiver. The Prowler has been developed through basic, expanded-capability, improved-capability and advanced-capability models, each featuring improvements to the electronic warfare equipment and the ALQ-99's computing power.

Prowlers were in action during the Linebacker II B-52 raids on Hanoi but, although impressed by the

The US Army's Grumman OV-1D Mohawk battlefield surveillance aircraft carries an array of photographic and electronic sensors in an under-fuselage pod.

concept, the USAF rejected an off-the-shelf purchase of the Navy aircraft because its speed and endurance would be inadequate over a European battleground. However, the Prowler's manufacturers, Grumman, were entrusted with the task of integrating its EW system into an airframe of appropriate size and performance—the General Dynamics F-111. The EF-111A is the result, rebuilt from 42 F-111A airframes and carrying the ALQ-99E tactical jamming system derived from the Prowler. Instead of pod mounting, however, the -99E has ten internal transmitters carried in a pallet in the weapons bay, radiating through an aerial array in a canoe housing beneath the fuselage. The receivers are housed in a number of fin fairings and resemble those on the EA-6B, but the USAF version of this powerful jamming system has reduced search time for the reception and identification of hostile signals, increased the number of threats that each jamming element can counter, and also increased operational flexibility by allowing omni-directional or directional transmissions via multi-mode antennae and through the use of a single signal source (exciter) by several jammers operating on different frequencies. A more capable central computer permits a greatly enlarged threat library and only one operator instead of three in the Prowler.

The manufacturers claim that a force of five EF-111As could radiate enough jamming power to affect most of the Warsaw Pact's air defence radars from the Baltic to southern Europe. Whatever the truth of this claim, the variable-geometry airframe affords great tactical advantages and allows three basic modes of operation. With wings straight the EF-111A can loiter in friendly airspace and fly racetrack patterns at an altitude where it will detect incoming enemy aircraft and jam their airborne intercept radars, while allowing friendly interceptors, AWACS and support aircraft to function freely. Again, the EF-111As could operate in a similar low-speed mode but at low level, flying orbits just behind the forward edge of the battle area and using their great jamming power to neutralize mobile SAM and radar-guided gunfire. Close air support orbits would be flown at low level and so-called battlefield air interdiction orbits at medium altitude in order to jam all air defence on the land or in the air.

With wings swept and flying supersonically, the EF-111A can perform its third type of mission, penetrating hostile airspace with a flock of strike aircraft while jamming air defence radars in a corridor leading to the assigned target. Electronic warfare is not exclusively concerned with the confounding of hostile search radars and weapons guidance systems. It can be developed to attack the decision-making brain of the enemy and the command control and communications (C^3) networks through which the electronic battlefield is animated. While devising means to dismember the opponent's C³ network, equal attention must be paid to protecting one's own.

The US Army and Air Force (latterly joined by the US Navy) are developing the Joint Tactical Information Distribution System (JTIDS), which replaces voice communication with high-volume pulses of coded digital information fired in short bursts, using rapid-frequency hopping for maximum jamming resistance. Terminals are being developed for installations on AWACS aircraft, on F-16 and F-15 fighters, and on RAF aircraft. When operational, JTIDS will give the combat aircraft pilot a complete overview of the land-air battlefield. He will be able to call up precise information on his location, the location of friendly forces and on developing air or ground threats.

Parallel to JTIDS are the USAF's Have Quick programme, designed to reduce the vulnerability of UHF voice communications to enemy jamming, and the longer-term Seek Talk programme which, by using random noise and spread-spectrum techniques, aims to keep UHF voice communication channels open, even in the most severe jamming.

Just as new offensive defence suppression weapons are entering service, a programme called Seek Screen is striving to reduce the vulnerability of the USAF's own tactical air control and missile radars to equivalent enemy attacks. Using technologies derived from the E-3A Sentry's radar, the Ultra Low Sidelobe Antenna programme aims to eliminate radar sidelobes (stray emissions of energy), thus making an attack by an anti-radar missile more difficult by confining it to the main radar beam. Meanwhile, Seek Screen's second element is an ARM alarm sensor

which, operating on a different frequency from the main radar it is protecting, will sense an impending attack and shut down the radar, denying the incoming ARM its guidance source. The third element of this advanced electronic counter-countermeasures programme involves decoys, saturating the target area with dummy emission sources.

Above and below: The U-2R and TR-1 are the latest developments of the U-2 extreme altitude reconnaissance aircraft first flown in the mid '50s. The U-2R is essentially an optical platform while the TR-1 with mission pods is a platform for electronic sensors.

CHAPTER 5

Air Power
at Sea

Sea warfare is now not just a matter of ship fighting ship. It is a highly complex interlocking battle above, on and under the sea, requiring composite forces of special-purpose surface warships, submarines, aircraft, satellites and electronics. Air power at sea is only a single, although vital, component, without which the winning of control of the sea and the exercise of sea power would be impossible.

The big aircraft carrier remains the primary instrument of maritime air power. It has, however, become the subject of marked controversy—whether it would survive in all-out warfare, whether it justifies its enormous expense or whether the resources it consumes would be better spread around a greater number of smaller hulls—and these are not just the concerns of the superpower navies.

During World War II the aircraft carrier established itself as the supreme arbiter of sea power. After 1945 naval air power assumed an important place in the early planning for nuclear war by the United States, Britain and, later, France.

Before the advent of long-range ballistic missiles, carrier aircraft were regarded as important means for bringing the Soviet Union within range of nuclear attack. In response the Soviet Navy, instead of attempting to match the Western alliance's carrier-borne strike power, developed and deployed large numbers of nuclear-powered attack submarines armed with cruise missiles as specialized 'carrier killers'.

Today only the United States can afford to build and put to sea the enormous concentration of military assets and trained manpower that a large nuclear-powered attack carrier (CVN) represents. The Royal Navy abandoned CTOL (conventional takeoff and landing carriers) with the scrapping of *Ark Royal* in 1980, but showed the flexibility and potential of V/STOL naval air operations from HMS *Invincible* and improvised merchant-ship platforms in the Falklands fighting of 1982.

France operates two conventionally powered CTOL carriers and has plans to replace them with nuclear-powered follow-ons by the end of the century. Navies such as those of Argentina, Brazil and India get by with aging hulls of early postwar vintage. Meanwhile, the helicopter has given many small navies and small ships the capability to operate aircraft either for anti-submarine warfare or for amphibious assault.

The technology of carrier aircraft

Fixed-wing carrier aircraft in service today are exclusively of US origin, with the notable exceptions of the British Sea Harrier, the Soviet Yak-36 Forger and the French Super Etendard. Today's generation was shaped by the requirements and the technology of 25 years ago—the US Navy wanted jets as good, if not better, than their supersonic land-based counterparts. The result was the F-4 Phantom II, which went on to become the most successful general-purpose combat aircraft since the war. The F-14 Tomcat, designed to be the F-4's successor, filled the gap left by the collapse of the naval F-111 programme in 1968 and remains one of the most capable co-interceptor aircraft in the world, land-based aircraft included.

Supersonic jet operations with large high-performance aircraft required bigger and bigger platforms. The logistic needs of large-scale conventional strike warfare in Vietnam saw carriers become huge floating bomb dumps rather than the nuclear delivery systems they had been considered to be in the 1950s. As carriers grew in size and a nuclear powerplant became almost obligatory, the smaller navies of the world, including the Dutch, Canadian, Australian and Royal Navy, were simply squeezed out by cost and either had to switch to land-based maritime airpower or look at the alternative that V/STOL offered.

The Falklands fighting showed how the remarkable Sea Harrier, armed with advanced AIM9L Sidewinder air-to-air missiles and flown by highly trained and competent pilots, could fight and win against theoretically superior supersonic land-based competition.

Supersonic V/STOL remains the unfulfilled goal of naval aircraft technology and it is here that the real challenge of the next generation lies. Ironically, it will require the economic and technological muscle of the United States to carry it through.

Naval aircraft have always imposed very special constraints on designers. Carrier aircraft have to be especially rugged to withstand the shocks of launch and arrested landing ('controlled crashes' as the US Navy calls them) and equipped with special hooks, shockproof undercarriages and low-speed handling control surfaces. Moreover, the airframe must be light and strong, yet resistant to the corrosive atmosphere on a carrier where salt water spray eats into aluminium and magnesium alloys. Dimensions are critical to be able to fit carrier deck lifts and hangar height, and the lifts and flight deck themselves impose weight limits.

A catapult shot punches the aircraft from zero to 140 knots in about 1·5 seconds and most of this load is on the nose wheel, where it engages the catapult. An arrested landing reverses the process, decelerating the aircraft from 130 knots to zero in 1·5 seconds. The severe stress imposed does not stop there. The sink rate of a typical naval aircraft landing is about 28 ft per second. As it hits the flight deck, the wing tips flex up, then momentum brings them down and they travel through an arc of two to three feet.

Carrier landing requires good low-speed performance but combat efficiency demands the best performance at high speed. High-altitude variable geometry is one answer but there is the penalty of weight and costs—the designer of naval aircraft has to find the right compromise. Naval aircraft also need long range and loiter time—to fit in with the carrier operating cycle, to mount combat air patrols for effective fleet air defence, or, in the case of surface strike aircraft, to make long over-water search and strike missions.

The advent of jet engines created new design complications. Piston engines driving variable-pitch propellers have a wide range of efficiency at various power settings. Jet engines, in contrast, have only two modes of operation—normal thrust, which provides power for supersonic flight, and afterburner, which is generally used only for short periods to blast the aircraft through Mach speed and beyond. Once the afterburner is lit, however, fuel is consumed at an enormous rate and for a small aircraft the effect on range is critical. This is why several significant carrier aircraft such as the A-6, A-7 and Super Etendard are subsonic.

The next generation of carrier aircraft

As will be seen, one of the arguments in favour of big CTOL carriers is the ability to operate comparatively large special-purpose aircraft, such as long-endurance fleet defence, anti-submarine and early-warning types. As V/STOL technology improves and simple devices like the 'ski jump' are incorporated into warship design, the old restrictions on useful load, range and fuel consumption will not prove so critical, and those who favour smaller carriers may find the

technical means to make them truly multi-purpose. The US Marine Corps A-V8B Harrier II (developed by McDonnell Douglas from the original British concept) has advanced aerodynamics and composite construction, giving it double the payload and range of the original AV-8A and making it comparable to the conventional F/A-18 in everything but speed. The real challenge facing naval aircraft designers is supersonic V/STOL but, in spite of many attempts, this concept has never entered the mainstream of naval policy making. Britain abandoned the supersonic P1154 Harrier development in 1965. The US Navy, under funding pressure, has cut back plans to test the Sea Harrier's radar in an AV-8B and to carry out experiments with an afterburning vectoring nozzle. Meanwhile the US Navy has drafted a requirement for a conventional take-off and landing aircraft (code-named VFMX) as a next-generation carrier aircraft to replace the F-14 Tomcat and A-6 Intruder in both the fleet defence and strike roles.

The US Navy and NASA do, however, have a STOVL technology-proving programme which could

The McDonnell-Douglas AV-8B, an extensive development of the original British Harrier, will begin to enter squadron service with the US Marine Corps in 1985.

The US Navy's carriers represent a massive concentration of strike power, but how long would they survive in all-out warfare? Each carrier air wing at present comprises 90-95 aircraft, including A-7Es, A-6Es, EA-6As and SH-3D helicopters seen here.

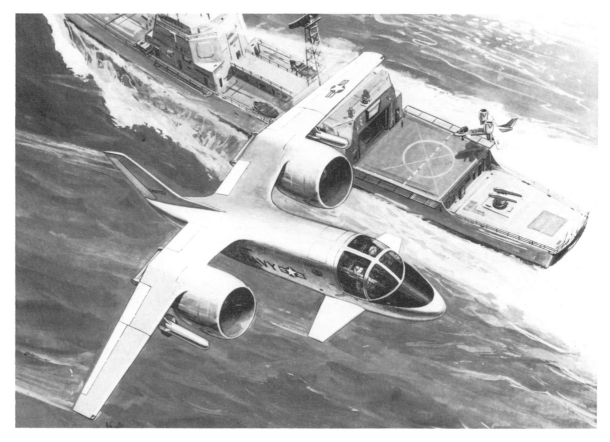

One of the advantages of big carriers is the ability to operate special-purpose types. This VTOL concept might give destroyer-sized ships that capability.

be put into effect in the event of a policy shift to small carriers. After eliminating proposals from Rockwell International and Vought in 1981, two design concepts are left in the running—from General Dynamics and McDonnell Douglas. The GD design, known as E-7, resembles an F-16 with chin intake and a delta wing but uses 'ejectors' installed in the wing roots and fed by the engine's fan stream to achieve V/STOL. In the centre rear fuselage is a single vectoring nozzle fed by the engine's core stream exhaust. In the cruise the fan stream exhausts through a conventional nozzle in the tail. The McDonnell Douglas 279-3 proposal uses four-nozzle vectored thrust in a close-coupled canard-winged airframe.

The role of air power at sea

Sea-based air power can be used to establish local sea control by deflecting enemy air or submarine attacks on friendly forces or it can be used to carry strike power to a distant enemy. A US strike carrier, for example, is constructed to carry specialized aircraft for these primary functions— airborne early-warning aircraft, dedicated air defence fighters to protect the carrier and its task group from air attack and intercept enemy land-based reconnaissance and missile-launching aircraft, anti-submarine warfare aircraft striving to screen the carrier and its escorts from underwater attack, conventional and nuclear-armed strike aircraft able to make long-distance attacks on enemy shipping or land forces, and, in addition, electronic warfare and tanker aircraft. The Royal Navy in the Falklands had, with slender resources, to fulfil the two vital tasks of securing sea control by deflecting attacks and of waging offensive strike warfare with a single type of aircraft, without the vital asset of airborne early warning (AEW). The remarkable Sea Harrier and its RAF equivalent, the Harrier G.R.3, hastily armed with Sidewinder missiles, both fought in the fleet defence role while making repeated low-level ground-attack missions.

Fleet air defence

The tactics and technology of fleet air defence have been evolved by the US Navy to meet the developing sub-surface, surface and airborne missile-firing threat presented by the Soviet Navy and Naval Air Arm. The Soviets developed a rudimentary integral air capacity in the early 1970s with the appearance of the Yak-36 Forger VTOL aircraft and the ships of the *Kiev* class but, if the reports of the Soviet Navy building a nuclear-powered CTOL carrier are correct, then by the late 1990s the world's oceans may see once again two carrier forces in the 1942 mould, each designed for attack on the other. Until then the primary role of the US carrier fleet is power projection and the securing of sea control through air superiority.

Fleet air defence, like virtually every other aspect of modern warfare, begins as a battle for the electromagnetic spectrum, with powerful shipborne radars and underwater sensors striving to pick up evidence of hostile forces and track their movements, while continually scanning for new threats. Because a sea-skimming cruise missile is much harder to shoot down than its launch aircraft, fleet air defence aircraft and missile systems have traditionally been structured to intercept the hostile launch platform as far out as possible and this means 'seeing' beyond the horizon. From 1942 onwards the US Navy began to develop airborne early warning for carriers, at first to observe enemy ships and aircraft at long range and then, more urgently, to counter the low-level threat of the Kamikazes.

Today's US carrier AEW aircraft, the Grumman E-2C Hawkeye, combines the functions of a powerful high- and low-level radar system with those of a flying combat information centre, able to direct fighter and strike operations over water or land. To ensure that an airborne AEW aircraft is in the air at critical times, however, a carrier needs to embark at least four of these comparatively large aircraft. Similarly, given the cramped conditions of a carrier deck and the pressures on the operating cycle, only a few dedicated interceptors can be maintained on combat air patrol

(CAP) at any one time. When pressures of this kind are taken into account, the arguments in favour of the huge supercarriers begin to become convincing.

The doctrine of combat air patrol dramatically illustrates the changing shape of fleet air defence in the age of missile warfare. Because an air-to-surface weapon can be launched at a range of 200 km or more, the launch platform must be intercepted beyond that range. The speed and agility of a sea-skimming cruise missile means that the traditional deck-launch intercept (DLI) is no longer enough. These scrambled alert aircraft on deck to meet a threat but, by the time the carrier was swung into wind and the engines fired, it might well be too late. An F-4 Phantom armed with Sparrow AAMs has to be 17 minutes out from the carrier to get in a first shot at an ASM-carrying Backfire.

The carrier's first line of defence, therefore, will not be surface-to-air missiles or DLI aircraft but fighters with their own very large radar capability, constantly orbiting 200 km out from the ship and armed with air-to-air missiles able to reach 75 km beyond that.

The Grumman F-14 Tomcat, with its very capable, large liquid-cooled Hughes AN/AWG-9 radar and weapons control system, plus long-range AIM-54 Phoenix missiles, is the chosen solution. The AWG-9

Another solution to the problem of getting integral airpower to sea without CTOL carriers is this ski-jump equipped tanker proposal from BAe with containerized air defence missiles.

If combat air patrol fighters fail to intercept a threat then point defence takes over. Here a Sea Sparrow Basic Point Defence Missile is being fired from a US carrier.

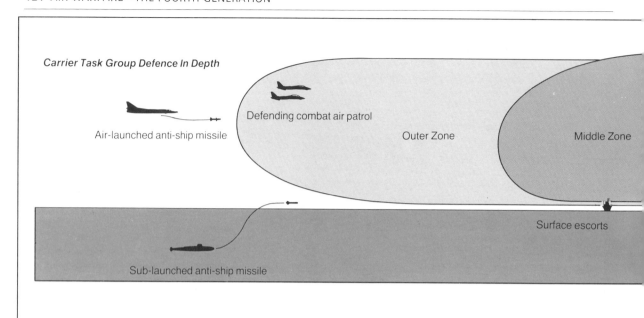

Carrier Task Group Defence In Depth

Air-launched anti-ship missile

Defending combat air patrol

Outer Zone

Middle Zone

Surface escorts

Sub-launched anti-ship missile

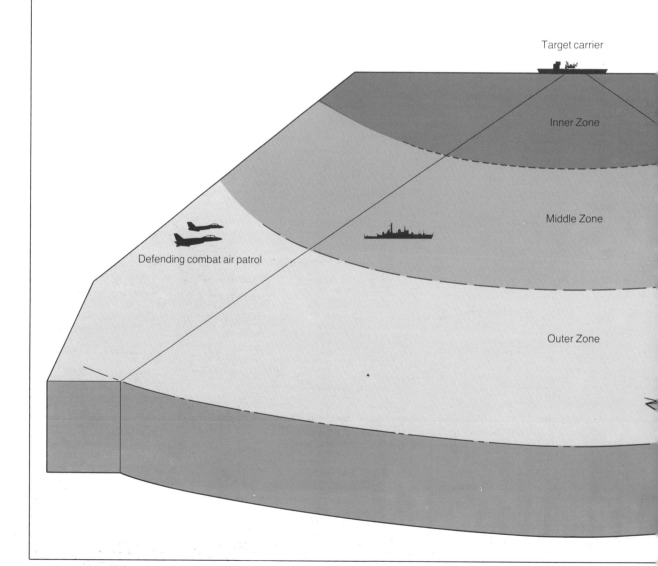

Target carrier

Inner Zone

Middle Zone

Defending combat air patrol

Outer Zone

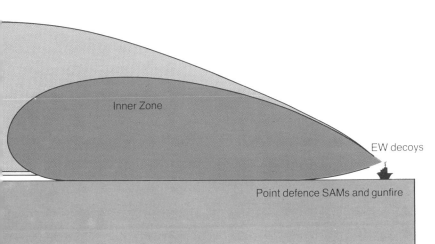

Inner Zone

EW decoys

Point defence SAMs and gunfire

Fleet air defence

Fleet air defence is not just a matter of shooting down hostile aircraft. Because they might be expected to make attacks with specialized anti-ship missiles, designed to skim the wavetops at high speed and equipped with radar for precision terminal guidance, a naval task force must defend itself in depth. There will be an outer zone of carrier-launched combat air patrol aircraft, themselves equipped with powerful long-range missiles, an inner zone of surface-to-air missile armed escorts and an inner zone of point defence, either by missile or by gunfire backed up by electronic countermeasures.

The US Navy, with its nuclear-powered supercarriers, is the most sophisticated exponent of fleet air defence in depth. Grumman F-14 Tomcat interceptors for, example, carry the Phoenix air-to-air missile, capable of very long range interceptions, extending the carrier's first line of defence effectively to some 250 km, aiming to shoot down attackers before they can launch their missiles.

With the Tomcats flying orbits some 180 km out from the ship, their missiles can reach out a further 70 km.

However, far out to sea it is judged more likely that an attack would be made with missiles launched from well over the horizon by submarines and surface ships, with land-based maritime reconnaissance aircraft, such as the Soviet Bear-D, providing the necessary radar guidance.

In such circumstances a small number of moderate-performance interceptors may prove effective, which provides the rationale for such aircraft as the Sea Harrier. If the launch aircraft or hostile submarine cannot be destroyed before launching its missile, then point defence is the last ditch.

Such missiles as the British Sea Wolf can even intercept shells in flight, while fast-slewing, rapid-fire rotary cannon such as the US Vulcan-Phalanx system can put a radar-directed wall of lead in the path of a sea skimmer. Electronic countermeasures, jamming, chaff and decoys are another last line of defence against a sea skimmer's own active terminal guidance radar.

It has been judged that eight strikes by sea skimmers with high-explosive warheads would be enough to sink a big aircraft carrier, although the Falklands experience when an Exocet, which in fact failed to explode, gutted HMS *Sheffield* has put new emphasis on point defence for surface warships and more effective damage control techniques

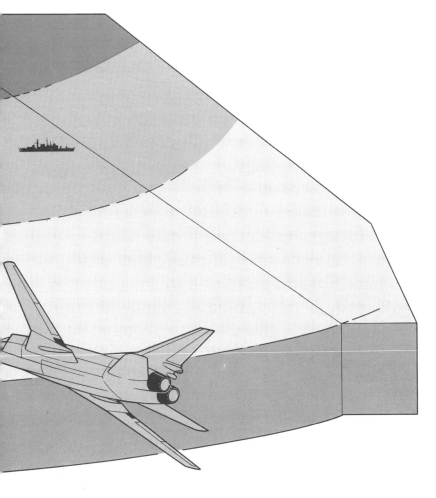

Opposite: The British Aerospace Seawolf is the Royal Navy's most modern short-range self-defence missile and acquitted itself well in the Falklands fighting, where no Seawolf-equipped ship was lost.

This page: The missile warfare underlined the need for close-in last-ditch defence systems such as the US Phalanx radar-directed, fast-slewing rotary cannon (*left*), which has been fitted on major Royal Navy warships.

The AM 39 air-launch version of the Exocet anti-ship missile under the wing of a French Navy Super Etendard. The combination proved devastating in Argentinian hands during the Falklands fighting.

Phoenix combination gave the Tomcat the world's first look-down, shoot-down capability, even against sea-skimming missiles. The Tomcat's radar can pick up targets at ranges up to 250 km and track 24 at once, while engaging six simultaneously. The AWG-9 provides the semi-active homing radar illumination for the big Phoenixes before their own terminal active radar takes over, although the problem of long-range IFF recognition remains.

Each Phoenix missile costs a third of a million dollars but is judged to be a cost-effective protection for billion-dollar task forces. Even so, the F-14 is limited in radar vision within which it can engage simultaneous targets and the Phoenix is now judged vulnerable to electronic countermeasures. Soviet land-based bombers such as Backfire, with new-generation anti-ship ASMs, put particular strain on the F-14 Phoenix combination, because there are too few to patrol on a 24-hour basis, and the cost in money, manpower and aircraft fatigue would be prohibitive. In areas of high threat a carrier will maintain several combat air patrols (CAP), with two fighters per station flying racetrack or figure-of-eight orbits. They are relieved in rotation without leaving gaps in coverage, and the relief aircraft must be ready on deck. Thus a US carrier with a Phoenix-armed CAP squadron of 12 F-14 Tomcats generally maintains two stations, with four aircraft as ready reliefs and four more undergoing maintenance at any one time.

In Vietnam, where US Navy aircraft in fact provided large ground-attack strike power, combat air patrols were mounted over target areas (TAR-CAPS) and as barriers (BARCAPS) to prevent enemy aircraft reaching the carriers or shore bombardment warships. In future, therefore, the lightweight dual-capable (strike warfare/air defence) F-18 Hornet will be employed on strike escort and barrier air patrol duties, while the less numerous F-14s remain on purely defensive combat air patrols, screening the fleet from long-range attack.

Strike warfare

The F/A-18 Hornet programme is a vital component of US Navy force modernization but the aircraft has increased in complexity and cost from the original concept of a lightweight multi-purpose fighter. After political threats to cut the programme unless the unit price was dropped, the manufacturers, McDonnell Douglas, brought the unit cost down to $22 million, and funding has been approved for another 63

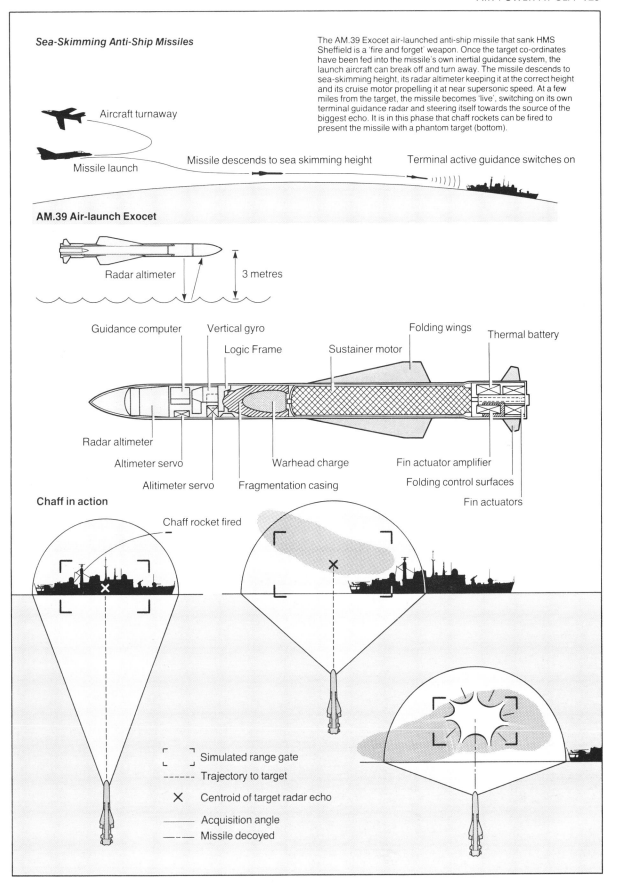

Sea-Skimming Anti-Ship Missiles

The AM.39 Exocet air-launched anti-ship missile that sank HMS Sheffield is a 'fire and forget' weapon. Once the target co-ordinates have been fed into the missile's own inertial guidance system, the launch aircraft can break off and turn away. The missile descends to sea-skimming height, its radar altimeter keeping it at the correct height and its cruise motor propelling it at near supersonic speed. At a few miles from the target, the missile becomes 'live', switching on its own terminal guidance radar and steering itself towards the source of the biggest echo. It is in this phase that chaff rockets can be fired to present the missile with a phantom target (bottom).

Aircraft turnaway

Missile launch

Missile descends to sea skimming height

Terminal active guidance switches on

AM.39 Air-launch Exocet

Radar altimeter

3 metres

Guidance computer

Vertical gyro

Logic Frame

Sustainer motor

Folding wings

Thermal battery

Radar altimeter

Altimeter servo

Alitimeter servo

Warhead charge

Fragmentation casing

Fin actuator amplifier

Folding control surfaces

Fin actuators

Chaff in action

Chaff rocket fired

Simulated range gate

Trajectory to target

X Centroid of target radar echo

Acquisition angle

Missile decoyed

The most significant naval aircraft of the 1980s will be the McDonnell-Douglas F-18 Hornet which, in spite of cost overruns, is destined to serve the US Navy in large numbers, replacing F-4s and A-7s.

Naval air power afloat

Argentina

The Comando de Aviación Naval Argentina operates 14 Super Etendards—the five that were on hand in May/June 1982 and nine subsequently delivered. Whether they will eventually operate from the navy's carrier *Veinticinco de Mayo* is questionable. The navy lost four A-4Q Skyhawks out of eleven in service and is receiving 24 ex-Israeli A-4E/Hs.

Veinticinco de Mayo (1945, commissioned in Argentine Navy, 1968).
Operates 21 aircraft, variable complement of A-4 Skyhawks, S-2A Trackers and Sea King ASW helicopters.

Brazil

Brazil's navy has operated helicopters afloat since 1968. The carrier *Minas Gerais*, commissioned in the Brazilian navy in 1960, is an ASW platform solely operating seven S-2A Trackers and four Sea King helicopters. Nine Lynx ASW helicopters are operated from six *Niteroi*-class frigates.

France

The two CTOL carriers, *Foch* and *Clemenceau*, underwent extensive refits in the early 1980s and will remain in service until the 1990s, operating Super Etendard aircraft in the strike and air-defence roles. Construction of a nuclear-powered carrier, the *Charles de Gaulle*, will, on present plans, start in 1986, with a second carrier to follow. The carrier-borne ASW aircraft is the Bréguet Alizé, which has undergone considerable modernization since its entry into service in the 1950s. *Clemenceau* (1961) and *Foch* (1963) carry 40 aircraft, Super Etendard/Etendard IVP.

India

The Indian navy's carrier *Vikrant* (ex-HMS *Hercules*, commissioned in 1961 after work suspended from 1946) has recently been modernized by the addition of a ski-jump. Six Sea Harriers have been delivered, with two more on order, replacing old Seahawks. The Indian navy operates Sea King helicopters in the ASW role and, for surface strike, Sea Eagle missiles are on order.

Italy

The Italian naval air arm has an ASW element of 28 Sea Kings deployed around various naval vessels. Some 16 Sea Kings will equip the new helicopter carrier, *Garibaldi*, when she enters service in 1984. Two squadrons operate AB 212 ASW helicopters based at Taranto and La Spezia.

Soviet Union

So far Soviet warships with air capability have been equipped as anti-submarine warfare platforms, carrying helicopters and small numbers of the relatively crude Yak-36 Forger VTOL aircraft for reconnaissance.

Helicopter cruisers
Moskva (1968)
Leningrad (1969)
Aircraft carriers
Kiev (1976) carries 20 V/STOL Forgers or 25 Ka-25 Hormone ASW helicopters
Minsk (1977)
Novorossiisk (1983)
one under construction

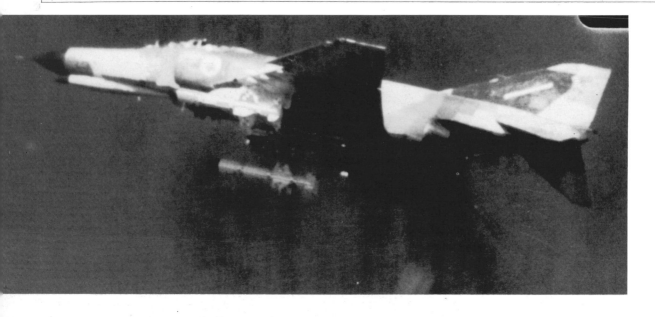

Spain

The Spanish navy became the third in the world to operate V/STOL aircraft at sea when it acquired eight AV-8As from the US Marine Corps in 1973. These operate from the ex-US aircraft carrier, *Dedalo*, which embarks seven AV-8A Matadors and up to 20 helicopters, Sea Kings or AH-1G Cobras. *Dedalo* will be replaced in 1984 by the *Principe de Asturias*, which is purpose-built from the US 'Sea Control Ship' design, has a 12° ski-jump and hangars for 20 aircraft. From 1986 the Matadors will be supplemented with 12 AV-8Bs and possibly the SH-60B in the ASW role.

Royal Navy

Plans to drastically run down the Royal Navy's air capability were reversed by the Falklands crisis and, by 1985, the Royal Navy's carrier force will consist of three ships, HMS *Invincible*, *Illustrious* and *Ark Royal*, the last replacing *Hermes* in 1985. Moreover, the successful operation of V/STOL aircraft from merchant ships opened up new experimental prospects. There are 24 Sea Harriers in service, with 14 on order to make up for losses. Deliveries are due to begin in mid-1985. At the same time, the aircraft in service will receive a mid-term systems update.

The Royal Navy's principal ASW helicopter is the Sea King, with 64 in service and more on order. Eleven Commando Sea Kings are in service, with eight more ordered. The Lynx is the principal air-to-surface vessel (ASV), helicopter-armed with Sea Skua missiles. There are 56 in service and 20 more are on order.

United States

The Reagan administration has sanctioned an increase in the US Navy from 13 carrier battle groups to 15, with a 600-ship navy by the 1990s. The 13th carrier, the nuclear-powered *Nimitz*-class *Carl Vinson*, became operational in 1982, with the fifth CVN, the USS *Theodore Roosevelt*, building and two more, CVN-72 and CVN-73, ordered from Newport News shipyards for delivery in 1989 and 1991. Each carrier operates an airwing of 90-95 aircraft.

CVN (nuclear powered aircraft carrier, year of commissioning in brackets)
Enterprise (1961)
Nimitz (1975)
Eisenhower (1977)
Carl Vinson (1983)
Theodore Roosevelt (1987)
CVN-72 *Abraham Lincoln* (1989)
CVN-73 *George Washington* (1991)
CV (conventionally powered aircraft carrier)
John F Kennedy (1968)
America (1965)
Constellation (1961)
Kitty Hawk (1961)
Independence (1959)
Ranger (1957)
Saratoga (1956)
Forrestal (1955)
Midway (1945)
Coral Sea (1947), used for contingencies and training)

Opposite: A Gabriel anti-shipping missile launched from an Israeli air force F-4. The Gabriel Mk III is a sea skimmer with a range of up to 60 km. *Above and right:* The US Harpoon is a very significant anti-ship missile, built in ship-, submarine- and air-launched versions. It can be launched from large land-based aircraft such as the RAF's Nimrod or USAF B-52Gs, as shown here, from the Lockheed S-3 (*left*) or Grumman A-6E. Harpoon uses mid-course inertial guidance, with active radar in the terminal phase.

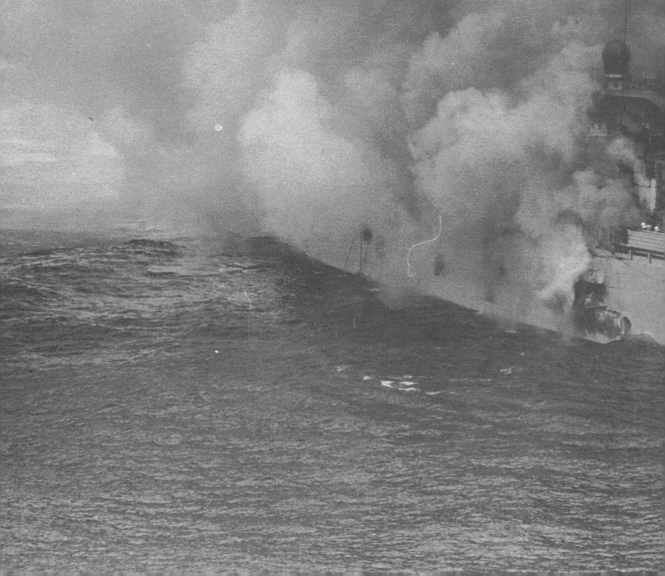

Main picture: HMS *Sheffield* blazes after having been struck by an air-launched Exocet. The missile in fact failed to explode, but unburnt fuel flashed fires which rapidly spread through the destroyer. *Left:* The lack of airborne early warning was sorely felt in the Falklands conflict. As a result Searchwater maritime surveillance radars have been tested in Sea King helicopters in the AEW role. The Royal Navy intends operating a flight of three Searchwater-equipped Sea Kings in each *Invincible*-class carrier.

aircraft in addition to the 63 already ordered. Armed with Sidewinder, Sparrow short- and medium-range air-to-air missiles and the M61 rotary cannon, the F-18 will replace the F-4 Phantom in the air defence role and, with the ability to lift over seven tons of ordnance, including precision-guided and tactical nuclear weapons, the Hornet will replace the A-7 Corsair II in the strike role. The whole programme could run to 1366 aircraft, with 316 Hornets for the US Marine Corps, 124 RF-18 reconnaissance variants and 146 attrition replacements.

Strike aircraft make up the bulk of a US Navy carrier air wing. Each carrier operates about 90-95 aircraft, made up of two squadrons (24 aircraft) of F-14As or F-4J/S for air defence, three attack squadrons—two with A-7 Corsair IIs and one with twelve Grumman A-6E Intruders, plus four KA-6D tankers. In addition, there is an electronic warfare support group of four EA-6Bs, an AEW squadron with four E-2C Hawkeyes, and an anti-submarine squad-

Left: Aérospatiale AS 330F Naval Super Puma, carrying two AM 39 Exocets. Exocets launched from helicopters have been used to attack shipping during the Iran-Iraq Gulf War.
Below: West German Navy Tornados carry the Kormoran air-launched anti-ship missile.

ron with ten Lockheed S-3A Vikings and eight SH-3D ASW helicopters.

The design of modern US carriers is dominated by the needs of strike warfare. As US military policy retreated from the massive nuclear threat and emphasized flexible response, so aircraft carriers became floating airfields. Massively laden with bombs and munitions, they were to be used for conventional warfare in Vietnam or planned conventional war in Europe, where US Navy aircraft would make strikes on Soviet tactical targets, supplanting land-based aircraft, which might have had their fixed-site airfields destroyed in the opening moves of a counter-air offensive.

While nuclear power gives a CVN virtually un-limited range, conventional strike warfare puts a heavy strain on logistic resources. An A-6 or A-7 carries over 5 tons of bombs on a typical mission and in a three-day high-intensity campaign will expend more than 45 tons. A strike air group of 36 will consume 1650 tons of air-to-ground munitions in three days.

While the need to carry very large amounts of rapidly consumed ordnance is another point in the supercarrier's favour, the advent of precision-guided, air-to-ground munitions and guided, sea-skimming anti-ship missiles has greatly increased the proba-bility of a given attack actually striking the target.

In examining fleet air defence much has been made of the threat of the sea-skimming missile and, because it has helped bring into being such important components of air-war technology as look-down shoot-down missiles and rapid-bloom chaff, it deserves a close scrutiny.

The Dassault Super Etendard carrier strike aircraft, which is just as effective if operated with Exocet from land bases. The type serves with France, Argentina and Iraq.

The sea-skimming missile is designed to present the smallest cross-section to a target warship's radar by hiding amidst the 'clutter' of the wave tops and the smallest target to last-ditch weapon systems by coming in fast and low. Typical examples use a radar altimeter for height keeping, inertial navigation for mid-course guidance and active radar homing for terminal guidance with a high explosive warhead or, in some cases, a nuclear warhead.

Missile warfare in the South Atlantic

Of the warships sunk in the South Atlantic fighting, only one, the *General Belgrano* was sunk by another warship—by a submarine-fired torpedo. The rest were sunk by air-to-surface action. Four were sunk or put out of action by 'iron bombs' (HMS *Antelope*, HMS *Coventry* and the logistic landing ships *Sir Galahad* and *Sir Tristram*), three were put out of action by helicopter-launched missiles (the submarine *Sante Fé*, and two Argentine patrol vessels), while an Argentine fishing vessel, strafed by Sea Harriers, surrendered. The frigate HMS *Ardent* was sunk by unguided rockets launched at close range by an Argentine MB339 strike/trainer.

But it was the stand-off missile attacks by Super Etendard aircraft armed with AM39 Exocet missiles which sank HMS *Sheffield* and the merchant ship *Atlantic Conveyor*. These missiles had a kind of cold, unstoppable terror about them and made a wide public aware of just how vulnerable surface warships are in the age of missile warfare. After the Falklands

McDonnell-Douglas F-18s in formation.

A trials F-18 with Marine Corps markings aboard a US aircraft carrier. A total of 270 F-18As are on order for the US Marine Corps.

experience the ships of the Royal Navy now bristle with newly installed close-in weapons systems (CIWS) as last-ditch defences against such missiles as the air-launched Exocet. Meanwhile, the navies (and the air forces) of the world strive to make sure they have drawn the right conclusions from what happened in the South Atlantic in May 1982.

Two days after the sinking of the *General Belgrano*, on Sunday May 2, the lead elements of the British task force, ploughing their way south, were now north of the Falklands and within the extreme range of land-based Argentinian strike aircraft. About 20 mi. ahead of HMS *Hermes*, the flagship, was HMS *Sheffield*, a 3500-ton Type 42 destroyer, armed with Sea Dart long-range area defence SAMs. As well as providing air defence for the fleet, Sheffield was to act as radar picket, using her type 966 masthead 'bedstead' radar to detect any hostile ships or air attacks before they threatened the main fleet.

Just before noon on May 4, Sheffield was at 'defence stations', the second state of combat readiness, giving the crew a break from the close-up discomforts of 'action stations'. The type 966 air-warning radar was temporarily shut down so as not to interfere with the transmission of a signal to Fleet HQ via communications satellite. Meanwhile, *Hermes* was providing a radar picture by way of the tactical data link.

Then from *Sheffield*'s operations room came the information that three aircraft targets had been identified but had been seen to turn away. It was assumed that they were Mirage IIIs probing the task force's defences and that they had declined to attack.

The assumption was terribly wrong. Suddenly the

electronic support warning equipment began to flash a signal that a radar had locked on to the ship. Again there was uncertainty as to whether it was hostile, since the computer's 'threat library' was programmed only to identify the electronic signatures of Soviet missiles as being dangerous. As the principal Warfare Officer realized what, in fact, was happening there was barely time to tell people to take cover.

An air-launched AM 39 Exocet missile fired by a Super Etendard had ripped into the destroyer's starboard side at the level of No 2 deck. The warhead had not exploded but the unburnt fuel in the missile and the heat of the impact had already started fires that spread through companion ways and cable runs, setting alight the main fuel tanks and sending clouds of toxic smoke from burning insulation and bedding through the ship, overwhelming all attempts to fight the blaze. After five hours, and with parts of the ship's plating now glowing white-hot, the order was given to abandon ship.

What had in fact happened? British Intelligence knew that Aviación Naval Argentina had received up to eight Super Etendards armed with AM39 Exocets and had pilots and technicians trained to fly and operate them.

With only eight Super Etendards available and perhaps as few as five missiles, Argentine plans for the use of these vital assets were crucial. Although the waters around the Falklands were full of targets, the Argentine Navy's surface fleet was bottled up by British nuclear-powered fleet submarines and the elderly carrier *Veinticinco de Mayo* could not come out even if she wanted to.

Initial planning apparently was for an air attack by two Super Etendards, operating from the airfield at Port Stanley itself. After Operation 'Black Buck', the Vulcan raid of May 1 and the much more effective Harrier raids and naval bombardment thereafter, the island base was judged to be too vulnerable.

Denied a forward operating base, the 2ª Escuadrilla de Ataque was obliged to plan a mission against the task force, flying at extreme range from Río Gallegos at the southern tip of the mainland. The attack radius of a Super Etendard armed with an AM 39 and with maximum internal fuel load is a modest 650 km. The attack, therefore, would need in-flight refuelling and here the Super Etendard's 'buddy pack' system would prove crucial.

By Monday May 3 three hand-picked pilots had been chosen to fly the mission. Faulty firing circuits had been detected and rectified and the complex electronic interfaces set up and aligned. At about 1045 on the morning of May 4 the three Super Etendards set off from Río Gallegos, some 470 mi. (750 km) from the Falklands.

Little over half an hour later, the three aircraft were within radar range of the task force. There is enough circumstantial evidence to suggest that they already had the approximate location of their targets (presumably the vital carriers, *Hermes* and *Invincible*) programmed into their ETNA inertial navigation system, based on intelligence derived from a submaritime sighting or from a high-flying maritime patrol aircraft such as a Lockheed SP-2H Neptune, tracking the task force on radar. This theory rests on the fact that the flagship *Hermes* picked up a high-level contact before the attack on Sheffield. There is, however, another explanation for this contact.

It could have been one of the Super Etendard themselves, briefly 'popping up' above the radar horizon to take a look with its own Agave attack radar. According to this supposition, the strike force formed up soon after takeoff and climbed to medium altitude in order to conserve fuel. As it came within radar range of the task force, two aircraft, each armed with a single AM 39, were topped up with fuel from the centre-line 'buddy pack' of the third Super Etendard. Now the formation descended to low level, to come in under the task force's radar. The third aircraft climbed and lost altitude at short intervals, turning on its radar momentarily to get the range and bearing of the target. The ETNA INS, meanwhile, handled the navigation, projecting steering commands on to the head-up display.

By now the aircraft were in battle formation, strung out about two miles apart, with the wing man a half mile behind the leader. The target co-ordinates from the radar reconnaissance aircraft were communicated by a secure data link and fed into the two fire-control systems. When the ETNA estimated the range at about 45 km, the pilots pulled up slightly to give the Exocet more room for release.

Each Exocet had to be energized before launch. The magnetron in the active radar nose needs a minute to warm up and the missile's own INS gyros need a further 36 seconds to be spun and aligned. The Exocet has a two-part guidance system. The carrier that launches a strike aircraft has its own sophisticated inertial navigation system—it 'knows' where it is, just as a land airbase is a fixed site. Before a mission these co-ordinates are fed into the strike aircraft's INS system. Thus, it 'knows' where it is at any point on the mission. The fire control feeds this information into the missile's own computer before launch and, because the missile automatically designates the point in mid-air from where it is launched, it can be given a set of co-ordinates and fly off to a mathematically predicted point in the sky without error and without any command link. It is electronically silent

Hornets in a low-visibility, two-tone grey paint scheme await their turn on the catapult aboard the USS *Enterprise*.

The British Aerospace Sea Harrier, Falklands veteran and the aircraft which has kept the Royal Navy's Fleet Air Arm in the business of fixed-wing flying. There are 24 in service with 14 more on order. Six are in service with the Indian Navy, aboard the carrier *Vikrant*.

until its own short-range homing head switches on, some five or six miles from the target. Now the missile is electronically 'live', hunting for its target by sending out electromagnetic energy and commanding itself to fly towards the biggest source of radar reflection as an air-to-air missile would do, except that a warship is bigger and slower-moving. It is only in this mode that the missile can be thwarted electronically, by firing clouds of chaff so as to present the missile with a phantom target.

An on-board radar altimeter looking at the sea keeps the missile skimming at just above wave height and, with a cruising speed of Mach 0.93, it is virtually impossible to shoot down. Its 364-lb (500-kg) hexolite warhead is devastating (although the warhead on the missile that struck *Sheffield* did not explode).

It is thought that the Argentine pilot flying the radar reconnaissance mission saw two blips on the Agave, one big and one small, presumably *Sheffield*,

Opposite: The US Navy's SH-60B Seahawk is described as the LAMPS III (Light Airborne Multi-Purpose System) acting in the anti-submarine role as a flying component of the ship. *Below:* Shipborne helicopters greatly extend the anti-submarine reach of surface escorts. This Aérospatiale SA 365 F carries ASW detection equipment, plus homing torpedoes and AS 15 missiles in the surface strike role.

with *Hermes* 20 mi. behind. Target co-ordinates were then transmitted to the missile-armed aircraft via a secure data link and the missiles were fired.

With the Exocets flying under their own power and under their own autonomous inertial navigation, the Super Etendards broke off, jettisoned their drop tanks and turned away, and this is what *Sheffield* interpreted as breaking off the action. In fact, two missiles were streaking towards the ship at just below the speed of sound. Even when the Exocet went 'active' and switched on its own homing head, the *Sheffield*'s ESM computer was not programmed to recognize the threat. The destroyer had five seconds left before impact.

On May 24 the Argentine Naval Air Force used the Super Etendards again in another attempt to sink the flagship *Hermes*. Two missiles were fired and the flagship reacted by firing clouds of chaff to defeat the Exocet's homing head. Altering course to centre on the new radar target, the missiles missed *Hermes* but then picked up the large container ship, *Atlantic Conveyor*, packed with vital war stores and three RAF Chinook heavy-lift helicopters. Two missiles struck, apparently both in the same place, but again only one exploded. The ship was ablaze and sinking and three seamen and the master were lost.

Air-launched anti-ship missiles

Argentina
MARTIN PESCADOR (KINGFISHER) Tactical short-to-medium-range air-to-surface missile, with range up to 9 km, compatible with fixed-wing strike aircraft or helicopters. May have armed A-4 Skyhawks for anti-ship strikes during Falklands conflict.

France
AS-12 Wire-guided missile with range of up to 8 km, for use by maritime patrol aircraft or helicopters for surface strike against small warships. Arms such types as 28 Nimrods and Bréguet Atlantiques, French Alouette III and Royal Navy Wasp and Lynx helicopters.
EXOCET AM39 The missile that sank the *Sheffield* and the *Atlantic Conveyor* in the Falklands fighting. Range is up to 70 km and speed high subsonic.

Germany (Federal Republic)
KORMORAN Development began in the late 1960s of this large anti-shipping missile to arm shore-based strike aircraft of the West German Navy. The guidance principle is the same as that of the Exocet AM39— inertial for mid-course and active radar for terminal homing. After lock-on, the missile descends to its final flight level, to hit the target just above the waterline. The warhead is 165 kg of high explosive designed to detonate once inside a warship hull, with special penetrators able to pierce up to seven bulkheads. The Kormoran arms West German Navy F-104Gs and is entering service on German Navy and Italian Air Force Tornados.

International
AIR-LAUNCH ANS The ANS (Anti-Navire Supersonique) is a joint Franco-Germany development programme for a successor to Kormoran and Exocet. The development missile is ramjet-powered and the specification calls for speeds of Mach 2 at sea level, high manoeuvrability and an autonomous guidance system.
MARTEL Joint Anglo-French air-launched anti-ship missile carried by French Atlantique and Mirage III aircraft, and by the RAF Buccaneer. Mid-course guidance is by auto-pilot. The AS 37 model uses hostile radiation from warship on which to home, and the AJ168 has a television camera and data link to the operator's position in the aircraft.
OTOMAT Franco-Italian development programme for an air-launch version of Otomat anti-ship surface skimmer. Could have range up to 200 km and two types of homing head, allowing either sea-skimming operation or climb and dive final attack.

Italy
MARTE Radar- or optically-guided 20-km range anti-ship missile for launch from helicopters of the Italian Navy.

Japan
ASM-1 Supersonic sea skimmer developed indigenously in Japan and arming Mitsubishi F-1 strike aircraft from 1982 onwards, compatible with updated F-4EJ Phantoms.

Norway
PENGUIN MK 3 Air-launch anti-ship missile, with range of up to 50 km. Has modified Bullpup warhead and is carried by F-16s of Norwegian air force. Is directed by inertial guidance to radar-mapped primary waypoint and then uses infrared terminal homing.

Sweden
RBS15 Development programme for dual air/surface launch anti-shipping missile with autonomous guidance system. Speed will be high-subsonic over long ranges at sea-skimming height.
SAAB 65A Radio command-guided tactical missile arming AJ37 Viggen aircraft in shipping and surface strike roles.
SAAB 04E Anti-shipping missile arming Viggen aircraft. After launch the missile is independent of the aircraft (unlike 95A), using an autopilot for mid-course guidance and an advanced homing head for precision terminal attack on a hostile warship.

Soviet Union
AS-1 AND AS-2 (KENNEL AND KIPPER) First-generation air-to-surface missiles of the late 1950s. AS-1 has 90 km range, the larger AS-2 has an estimated 200 km and may be nuclear-armed, although primarily an anti-shipping weapon. Carried by Tu-16 Badger.
AS-5 KELT Rocket-propelled anti-shipping weapon with range around 160 km +. Guidance in mid-course is inertial, with active radar terminal guidance. A passive radar-homing anti-radiation version has been reported. In service on Badgers of Soviet Navy and Egyptian Air Force.
AS-4 KITCHEN Advanced, dual-purpose, air-launch missile, strategic version with 200-kiloton nuclear warhead and shipping strike conventionally armed version. Arms Tu-22 Blinder, Tu-22M/Tu-26 Backfire and Tu-95 Bear.
AS-6 KINGFISH High-performance, anti-ship missile arming Soviet naval Tu-16 Badgers. Has supersonic speed in cruise and diving terminal attack.

The Bréguet Atlantique Nouvelle Génération packs
completely updated electronics into a proven airframe to
provide a land-based maritime patrol aircraft of high
capabilities.

United Kingdom

SEA SKUA All-weather, small sea-skimmer arming
shipborne helicopters for attacks on surface ships.
Guidance employs semi-active homing up to 15 km
range. The system proved effective in the Falklands
fighting.

SEA EAGLE Planned to succeed the Martel on RAF
Buccaneer and Tornado strike aircraft and on the
Sea Harrier as primary British air-to-surface anti-
ship weapon. Range will be more than 100 km. Will
have advanced active radar homing with over-the-
horizon capability. Ordered by Indian Navy.

United States

MRASM Medium-range, air-to-surface development of BGM-109 Tomahawk sea-launched cruise
missile. Can be adapted for conventional land
attack or anti-shipping strike. Guidance is mid-
course inertial, with TERCOM refinement and
digital scene area matching for terminal guidance.

BULLPUP Short-range, command guidance weapon
which entered service with US Navy in 1959. Has
been used by various NATO navies including Royal
Navy Buccaneers but is no longer in US service.

WALLEYE There are three models of unpowered
guided bombs in the Walleye series for land or sea
attacks on land or naval targets. The weapon has a
TV camera in the nose which locks on to a target
designated by the pilot and autonomously steers the

free-fall weapon on to it. Walleye can carry a large
(907 kg) conventional or nuclear warhead.
Principal launch aircraft is A-7.

NAVY MAVERICK Development programme for
precision-guided 'powered bomb' to arm A-7s,
A-6Es and F/A-18s of the US Navy from 1984
onwards for strikes against land targets or warships. Differs from the USAF's TV- and laser-guided
maverick by using imaging infrared which can
distinguish a warship at night or in adverse
weather.

HARPOON The McDonnell Douglas-developed Harpoon is now officially regarded as the US Navy's
primary anti-ship weapon and comes in surface-
ship, submarine- and air-launch variants. Large
numbers are on order for the US and other navies.
The guidance principle is the same— the missile is
given target information by the launch platform's
fire control, inertial guidance takes it to the scene of
action, while a radar altimeter secures sea-
skimming station keeping. Terminal guidance is
provided by a Texas Instruments DSQ-28 active
radar-homing system, which maintains its lock
until final impact. The air-launched Harpoon
entered service on P-3 Orions in 1979 and on the
A-6E and A-7 in 1981-2. The missile is compatible
with a number of other aircraft including the F/
A-18, the S-3 Viking ASW, certain helicopters, the
F-111C and RAF aircraft such as the Nimrod.

The RAF's Nimrod MR 2s provide long over-water surveillance capability and can be armed with depth charges, anti-ship missiles and even Sidewinder AAMs for self-defence, as in the Falklands fighting.

Land-based maritime air

As will be seen from the above table several large, slow, long-endurance aircraft are designed to carry anti-ship missiles or provide mid-course over-the-horizon guidance data for missile-firing submarines, although they could not be expected to survive in areas of high threat. Land-based maritime air, however, includes high-performance strike aircraft such as the Buccaneer, Tornado and Swedish Viggen. They have the speed and weapons systems to strike heavily defended targets and are based so as to be able to intervene decisively in areas of strategic importance, such as the Greenland-Iceland-UK (GIUK) gap, the eastern Mediterranean or the Baltic. From the Argentine point of view, for example, the air-sea warfare in the South Atlantic was waged by aircraft operating from land bases.

The primary uses of land-based maritime air are reconnaissance and anti-submarine warfare. There are large numbers of long-endurance patrol aircraft in service with western navies and air forces, with a global reach able to provide a tactical picture of what is happening on and, to some extent, under, the world's oceans. During the Falklands crisis, the Argentines used an air force Boeing 707-300 to shadow the British task force's progress south. Types in service include the Bréguet Atlantique, the Japanese Shin Meiwa flying-boat, the Canadian CP-140 Aurora, the Lockheed P-3 Orion, the Nimrod MR 2, and dwindling numbers of Lockheed P-2 Neptunes. The Argentine air force is reworking second-hand L-188 Electra airliners with Israeli-supplied avionics for maritime patrol USAF B-52s and, in the early 1980s, RAF Vulcans were rotationally committed to maritime surveillance.

The Soviet Union is reported to have put the veteran Tu-95 Bear turboprop-powered patrol bomber back into production, so useful are the endurance and range capabilities of this aircraft in the maritime reconnaissance role. The M-4 Bison serves in the maritime reconnaissance role, as does the Be-12 Mail flying boat.

Meanwhile, in the last few years a new class of military aircraft has grown up to serve in the maritime sovereignty enforcement role, with many of the world's smaller air forces providing an active market. Often based on a short-haul airliner airframe and designed for maximum economy of operations, such aircraft may be armed or unarmed. Types include the British Coastguard, based on the HS 748, the Fokker F.27 capable of 12-hour maritime patrols on twin engines, the Brazilian EMB-111A, and the Britten-Norman Defender, the French Dassault Gardien Maritime and the Australian GAF Searchmaster L. The Indonesian Navy, for example, uses its Searchmasters on inshore work around thousands of islands in its efforts to fight piracy.

Aircraft versus submarine

NATO's anti-submarine warfare strategy is a result of history and geography. At the time when large numbers of wartime convoy escort vessels were approaching the end of their lives, the US Navy developed and deployed the SOSUS system, large arrays of passive hydrophones which could detect the passage of a submarine across an oceanic basin at very long range, with primary cover of the Atlantic. With the ability to fix the position of hostile submarines but without large numbers of escort warships, the convoy strategy was abandoned for all but critical military targets, and an offensive strategy based on long-range air power put in its place. Guided by a SOSUS contact, a US Navy P-3 Orion could start a local hunt for a submarine by sowing a pattern of sonobuoys, reading their signals with large on-board computer power and, after confirmation of a submarine contact with magnetic anomaly detectors, making attacks if necessary with homing torpedoes or nuclear depth-bombs. The SOSUS-offensive maritime air combination depends on slow progress in efforts by the Soviets to make their large number of attack submarines quieter-running or equip them with effective anti-aircraft self-defence weapons.

The shipborne helicopter is the principal anti-submarine system of ASW escorts. It vastly extends search range and the ship's offensive reach, and provides over-the-horizon, surface-to-surface targeting. In the case of the US Navy's LAMPS Mk III (Light Airborne Multi-Purpose System), based on the Sikorsky SH-60B, the helicopter acts as a flying component of the ship. It is tied by secure data link to its computer and sensor power and able to respond to the ship's own long-range sonar contacts at ranges up to 160 km.

Above: The Lockheed P-3C Orion is the US Navy's standard land-based maritime patrol and ASW aircraft. In Canadian service it is designated CP-140 Aurora.

Below: Dassault-Mystère Falcon 20 Gardian, originally designed as an executive jet, has been developed into an effective coastal surveillance aircraft.

CHAPTER 6

Transport
Aircraft

The great colonial empires of the past were held together militarily by sea power. It served to keep out rivals and could transport an expeditionary force from the mother country to the aid of an embattled local garrison, although it might take months to do it.

The empires are gone and in their place are the superpowers, facing each other down with their nuclear deterrents, but bound by regional alliances and perceptions of their security needs to military commitments all over the world.

The zones of maximum US military sensitivity are in Europe, in the Middle East, Israel and South West Asia, in South Korea and latterly in Central America, all thousands of miles from the continental United States. The Soviet Union guards its land borders with NATO and with China. It has to rotate its huge garrisons in eastern Europe and is embroiled in war in Afghanistan. Meanwhile, Soviet power has filled the vacuum left by colonial retreat with opportunist power projection wherever circumstances seem favourable— in South East Asia, Africa, the Caribbean and beyond.

The huge load carrying capacity of the C-5 is apparent from this picture. A huge rewinging programme will extend the fleet's capabilities.

The classic instrument of power projection remains sea power, but in the eyes of the superpowers and some would-be world powers the ability to apply military force globally in a matter of hours rather than weeks is an imperative of perceived security needs and that means airlift. In the Oct. 1973 Middle East war, for example, US C-5 and C-141 transport aircraft delivered over 22,000 tons of vitally important military supplies to Israel in 33 days. The first ship arrived with more tonnage, but by then the war was over.

Most of the air forces of the world have squadrons dedicated to military transport— more often than not flying the ubiquitous Lockheed C-130 Hercules. In spite of the dominant position of the Hercules in world markets, there are (excluding the Soviet Union) several other significant tactical transport types in worldwide service, such as the Franco-German Transall, the Italian Aeritalia G222, the Japanese Kawasaki C-I and the Canadian DHC-6 Buffalo. Meanwhile, many veteran US transports from the C-47 onwards continue in service with minor air forces.

Between them the United States and Soviet Union together account for more than 80% of all military airlift— much of the Soviet capacity being deployed for military mobility within the vast wastes of the Soviet Union itself. For strategic long-range operations, the United States has the Civil Reserve Air Fleet (CRAF) to draw on, with 123 long-range cargo and 250 passenger aircraft, which can augment the capabilities of Military Airlift Command (MAC) as required. Aeroflot, the state carrier of the Soviet Union and the world's largest airline, is fully integrated with Soviet Air Transport Aviation (Voenno Transportnaya Aviatsiya V-TA). Its pilots are military reservists and its commander is a Soviet air marshal. Aeroflot's transports are technically interchangeable with military types and, if required, could increase troop-carrying and cargo capacity by a third.

There is a narrow dividing line between the elements of tactical and strategic airlift, looked at below. Strategic operations imply long-range lifts in secure airspace, with aircraft configured like airliners, for operations from long, hardened runways. Tactical operations imply shorter hops, landing in disputed areas on shorter, rugged airstrips, or operations with paratroops or air-landing infantry. Heavy-lift and assault helicopters have assumed many of these battlefield-mobility and amphibious roles.

The United States began to develop the forces for an ocean-spanning strategic military airlift during World War II when its military forces were committed at either side of the U-boat-infested Atlantic and the equally inhospitable Pacific Ocean. Such types as the C-54 and C-69 were demilitarized in 1945 as the DC-4 and Lockheed Constellation, to pioneer the kind of worldwide intercontinental airline operation we

Above: The C-5A's wheel landing gear is designed to spread the aircraft's great weight and provide flotation on soft landing fields.

Below: Rewinged C-5s, reworked to C-5B standard, are emerging in a new and purposeful paint scheme which does little to make the machine less ugly.

If the C-5's huge size needed underlining this shot of a Galaxy being tanked by a KC-135 shows off the sheer scale of this enormous aircraft.

A C-141B of the USAF's Military Airlift Command dropping paratroops and their equipment directly into action after a long transoceanic flight.

know today. The Berlin airlift of 1948 showed the strategic importance of military air transport, even in the new age of atomic weapons.

As the United States abandoned the tripwire/ massive retaliation strategy of nuclear deterrence and became involved in an expanding alliance system, the 'POMCUS' concept grew. This was the placing in position beforehand of heavy equipment and bulk military supplies outside the continental United States, ready to be united, during a crisis, with the troops who would use them. Western Europe was the most important consideration, but US forces were pre-positioning supplies in Turkey for possible operations in the Middle East as early as 1958.

Without pre-positioning the problems of strategic airlift are considerable. For example, in the planning for the US Rapid Deployment Force, (now renamed Central Command), which is expected to arrive and be ready for combat in an area of maximum military tension, it was calculated that 700 equivalent sorties by C-141 Starlifter would be required to lift the combat elements of a light airborne division with a basic load of ammunition plus five day's rations and fuel, from the US eastern seaboard to the Gulf.

US airlift
US Military Airlift Command (MAC) superseded the original Military Air Transport Service (MATS) in

1966 and took over tactical transport in 1975. It now directs almost 1000 aircraft from 13 major airbases in the United States, operates the mid-Atlantic staging-post at Lajes in the Azores and the main European terminal at Rhein-Main AB outside Frankfurt in West Germany. MAC includes the Air Weather Service, the Aerospace Rescue and Recovery Service and the Aeromedical Airlift Wing, all based at MAC HQ, Scott AFB, Illinois. Two Air Forces, 21st (McGuire AFB, New Jersey) and 22nd (Travis AFB, California) incorporate 13 squadrons flying 268 C-141Bs and four squadrons with 77 C-5A Galaxies. The programme to 'stretch' the C-141 to B-configuration, with the addition of 30% increase in bulk cargo capacity, plus in-flight refuelling, is complete and a major wing modification to the C-5 fleet will be complete by 1987.

The Galaxy is an extraordinary aircraft, still 15 years after its first flight an expression of US technical ability and military power. There have been problems. Although it was originally designed to carry two tanks, the standard load is a single tank because of wing structure deterioration and 17% have been out of service at any one time. After several costly modification programmes have failed to provide a solution, the entire fleet will be re-winged, to add 30,000 hours of aircraft service life. The wing problems also increased runway length requirements, which are a very important consideration for military transport operations. C-5s and C-141s can operate only from 25% of airstrips in Europe,

The projected McDonnell Douglas C-17A is designed to combine the payload of a C-5 with the tactical short-field performance of a C-130.

constrained by lack of runway length, load-bearing capacity, parking facilities, instrument landing facilities, airfield lighting and so on.

Throughout the 1970s the USAF had a requirement for a pure-jet short takeoff and landing replacement for the C-130 tactical transport. With the new emphasis on the Rapid Deployment Force and the need to project power at global ranges directly into action, the USAF dropped the original requirement which produced the YC-14 and YC-15 ASMT (advanced, short takeoff military transport) prototypes. It issued a new 'C-X' request for proposals

The C-141A Starlifter was designed around the same fuselage cross-section as the C-130 Hercules. An extensive programme has been completed to stretch the fleet to C-141B standard and incorporate in-flight refuelling receptacles.

which would produce an aircraft combining the C-130's short-field capability with the cargo capacity of a C-5. The McDonnell-Douglas solution to this highly taxing technical problem, typenamed C-17A, was selected in 1981.

The programme did not last long. Faced with huge uncertainties over costs, the US government became reticent about the C-17, while Congress was suspicious of an aircraft that could lift only a single M-1 Abrams tank. To fill the gap the USAF has recommended to the Department of Defense the procurement of 50 new C-5Bs and 44 KC-10 tanker transports.

In 1982 MAC purchased eight ex-American Airline Boeing 707 airliners, designated C-18As, to keep up its people-moving capabilities (it carries almost two and a quarter million passengers in a year). Six squadrons fly C-9As (virtually identical to the civil DC-9-30 airliner), with a VIP flight of three VC-9As based at Andrews AFB, near Washington. Five VC-137Bs and Cs, also assigned to the 89th Military Airlift Group at Andrews AFB, provide presidential and senior national executive transport, 11 C-135B/C Stratolifters and, for weather reconnaissance, deploy two WC-135Bs and 13 WC-130s. These specially converted Hercules can enter tropical storms in order to gain data on their behaviour and forecast their movements.

Although it was first ordered for the USAF over 30

The Lockheed C-130 Hercules remains the workhorse of USAF's tactical air transport squadrons and many other air forces.

years ago, the C-130 remains in production and provides the platform for a very wide range of further specialized roles. There are some 270 C-130 Es and Hs, flying with 14 active units. The supporting Air National Guard and Air Force Reserve inventory has 14 groups and five wings of some 250 older models. Reliance on reserves has increased markedly since 1970, when 394 C-130s were assigned to active squadrons.

Although the C-130's cargo compartment is too small to take the new generation of US Army M2 and M3 Infantry/Cavalry Fighting Vehicles, no replacement tactical transport was waiting in the wings once the ASMT programme was cut back.

MAC is responsible for the Aerospace Rescue and Recovery Service (ARRS), which has the task of combat search and rescue, weather reconnaissance, air sampling, drone recovery, SAC missile site support and Space Shuttle emergency support. The ARRS flies HC-130, WC-130 and WC-135 aircraft, together with various models of the HH-1, HH-3, HH-53, and UH-1 helicopters. An initial batch of nine UH-60A Nighthawk combat rescue helicopters has been delivered to MAC, with a stated requirement for more than 230 more. Four ARRS squadrons are found by the Air Force Reserve.

Soviet airlift

V-TA, the Soviet equivalent of Military Airlift Command, is a vital component of Soviet military power, operating some 1200 strategic and tactical aircraft, ranging in capacity from the outsize An-22 Cock to the biplane An-2 Colt. Because of poor lines of land communication, airlift has always been important both internally, for the rotation of garrisons in eastern Europe, and for the tactical support of any military operation on Soviet Warsaw Pact frontiers, including Afghanistan. Throughout the 1970s the Soviet Union was developing a longer reach. In Oct. 1973, 225 Soviet aircraft flew 15,000 tons of military supplies into Arab states. A logistic link was forged with Angola in 1975, and direct flights were made into Ethiopia in 1977-8 and into Vietnam during that country's confrontation with China. The Soviet invasion of, and continued war in, Afghanistan, beginning in Dec. 1979, has been very largely supported by military airlift.

The shortage of prepared airfields both at such Third World destinations and in Siberia has meant that Soviet transports are designed for rough-strip short takeoff and landing operations — with, for example, such features as high power-to-weight ratios, multi-wheel undercarriages, adjustable tyre pressure, rocket-assisted takeoff, etc. There are also such simple provisions as on-board generators and fuel pumps to free them from reliance upon ground equipment. In addition, Soviet transport aircraft often fly with an extra crew of maintenance personnel.

Soviet paratroops boarding their massive Il-76 Candid transports. The aircraft has good performance on short, austere airstrips. *Opposite, top left:* the US Department of Defense published this impression of the massive An-400 Condor transport at the beginning of 1984. The strategic implications of being able to rapidly redeploy missiles such as the SS-20 causes particular concern.

The McDonnell-Douglas KC-10A Extender is a reworking of
the DC-10 airliner, designed to give the USAF an advanced
tanker/transport aircraft, significantly increasing the ability to
deploy tactical air power over long ranges. Procurement has
been cut back by funding restraints.

Above: The Franco-German Transall tactical transport is one of the few contenders in the C-130 Hercules area. The aircraft is in production again with in-flight refuelling capability.

Below: The Outsize Soviet An-22 has been a relative failure operationally, with few in service and a string of crashes. It can accommodate tactical missiles and tanks.

In developing really big airlifters, the Soviet Union has been restricted by its lack of the equivalent technology of large US turbofan engines. The turboprop-powered An-22 Cock, equivalent to the C-5, can lift outsize loads such as tanks and surface-to-air missile systems, but production stopped in 1974 and more than a few have been lost in crashes. It is reported that a turbofan-powered heavy-lift strategic transport aircraft, type-named An-400 Condor, is under development to replace the 50 or so An-22s.

The Ilyushin Il-76, first flown in 1971, bears a resemblance to the C-141 but has greater short-field capability, although not in-flight refuelling. The Antonov An-12 Cub again bears a superficial resemblance to the Hercules but is judged inferior in most critical respects. However, the fleet of over 500 An-12s can accommodate all the equipment, including armoured vehicles, assigned to Soviet airborne divisions and 60 aircraft could lift the 1500 tons payload of a mechanized battalion. The Antonov An-24 and An-26 (Coke and Curl) are shorter-range twin-engined transports, serving in comparatively small numbers, and will eventually be replaced by the pure-jet An-72 Coaler, designed for optimum short-field performance. Some 30 Ilyushin Il-18 Coots serve as basic troop transports, while liaison and VIP work is handled by Yak-40 Codlings and Tu-134/154s, with two or three Il-62s adapted for VIP work.

Great Britain progressively ran down its strategic airlift capability as its world role contracted to become a regional NATO military commitment. The last long-range military airlifters, the small fleet of Short Belfasts, were sold off to civil operators in the late 1970s and, during the Zimbabwe peacekeeping operation of 1980, extensive use was made of US-supplied strategic airlift. Suddenly, in the spring of 1982, Britain had to make a response to a military challenge in the Falkland Islands at the other end of the world.

Travelling the distance involved, 13,000 km

A C-9 Nightingale of US Military Airlift Command, able to accommodate 40 stretcher patients. The aircraft is based directly on the DC-9-30 airliner.

(8000 mi.), would be akin to sending a task force from London to Tokyo. The single staging-post, Wideawake airfield on Ascension Island, was virtually halfway, but this would be like having to use Bombay as the first and only staging post to Japan.

In the initial invasion, Argentinian C-130s flew in troops and supplies and, during the early stages of the British enforcement of the exclusion zone, they continued to get into Port Stanley at night. One Argentinian C-130 was shot down by a Sea Harrier on June 1 but it had to use two Sidewinders and all its 30-mm ammunition to accomplish this. The Argentinians used C-130s as bombers on two occasions, rolling bombs off the cargo ramp to attack shipping. Both attacks were unsuccessful.

The RAF's long-range transport is the operational concern of Strike Command and involves No 10 Squadron at Brize Norton, with 13 VC-10s and the C-130 Hercules wing at Lyneham of 24, 30, 47 and 70 Squadrons. Of the 60 Hercules in RAF service in early 1984 (out of 66 originally purchased from the United States when development of the indigenous HS tactical transport was abandoned in 1966), the wing has six C.1K tankers, and C.1P receivers fitted with refuelling probes. Some 30 aircraft are being stretched, with a fuselage extension of 4·57 m. Throughout the period of conflict in the South Atlantic, RAF Hercules provided 13,000 hours out of a huge total of 17,000 hours of airlift to Ascension and then into Stanley itself, in flights which required multiple-stage in-flight refuelling. Flights from Ascension to the Falklands and back, air-dropping supplies without landing averaged over 25 hours and one (by a C-130 of 70 Squadron) lasted 28 hours, 3 minutes. The first RAF Hercules C-130 was actually able to land at Stanley, two weeks after its capture, once mines had been cleared.

CHAPTER 7

Strategic Bombers

For a time after 1945 the strategic long-range bomber, the aircraft that had dropped the atomic bomb, was the most important type of aircraft in the world. But two things had come of age in the last years of World War II— atomic weapons and an apparently invulnerable and unstoppable delivery system, the ballistic missile, the combination of which would eventually topple the bomber from its pedestal. The first effective surface-to-surface missile with an appropriate strategic range was the German Army's V-2 rocket, and captured examples were eagerly examined after the war by technicians in the United States, the Soviet Union and Britain. Missiles with intercontinental range were still a long way off and another avenue of German technical research was explored just as eagerly— jet propulsion, with its application to bombers in particular.

During the second half of the 1940s the United States and the Soviet Union developed jet-powered medium-range bombers, significant types being the B-45 Tornado, the XB-47 Stratojet, and the Soviet Tu-14 Bosun and Il-28 Beagle. The British Canberra prototype flew in 1949 and the French Vautour in 1952. However, the real challenge was the application of the new jet technology to large aircraft with intercontinental ranges, capable of striking the heartland of each of the new postwar superpower rivals. The key USAF bomber of the period was the B-47, very large numbers of which entered service from 1951 with Strategic Air Command (founded in 1947). Like their equivalents in the equally new and

The USAF's ageing fleet of B-52s has been the subject of continuous engineering and electronic updates to keep them in the front line since the late 1950s. Just over the crew members' shoulders can be seen the computer graphics display for new terrain-avoidance radar installed in the well-used cockpits of B-52Gs and Hs in 1984.

Above and below: These USAF artist's concepts of the late 1970s give little clue as to the true shape of the Advanced Technology Bomber (ATB), incorporating so-called 'stealth' technology, which, on present plans will supplant the B-1B as the USAF's manned penetrating strategic delivery system in the 1990s.

An FB-111A of Strategic Air Command reveals an internally stored SRAM (Short-Range Attack Missile).
Opposite, left: A SRAM lights up after falling free of the aircraft. SRAM can fly preprogrammed flight paths on inertial guidance and deliver a nuclear warhead equivalent to a Minuteman III ICBM re-entry vehicle.

Main picture: A B-52G drops an ALCM (Air-Launched Cruise Missile). A proportion of SAC's veteran B-52 force are being reworked as cruise missile carriers, able to carry 12 ALCMs on underwing pylons (*inset left*). Meanwhile over 1000 SRAMs (*inset right*) remain in the inventory.

Armourers tend the pylon-mounted ALCMs of a B-52G. The first cruise-missile carrying squadron became operational at the end of 1982.

independent Soviet long-range aviation (DA, founded in 1948) which could not reach the United States, the B-47s could not reach the Soviet homeland except from forward bases in Western Europe or North Africa. As a result the United States never abandoned the forward military position it had won in the war and, when NATO was formed in 1949, the pattern of confrontation in Europe was set.

There was a bomber in the US armoury that could reach and drop atomic weapons on Soviet soil if necessary. This was the extraordinary Convair B-36 Peacemaker, powered by six piston engines driving pusher propellers, assisted by four podded turbojets. It could cruise at an altitude beyond that of contemporary interceptors and was designed to carry a bombload of 10,000 lb over 10,000 mi. The new independent Air Force won a bitter funding battle with the US Navy in 1948 over its efforts to get its $6 million wonder aircraft into service.

Just as the B-36's replacement, the exceptional Boeing B-52, was entering service in 1955, guided missile research was progressing in two very important directions. One result of this was the big surface-to-air radar-guided missile which made operations at high altitude anything but safe. The second was the missile with truly intercontinental range, tipped with a thermonuclear weapon of great destructive power. Faced with high-altitude SAMs and supersonic interceptors, it seemed as if the day of the big bomber, cruising serenely at high altitude, was fast ending. At the same time supersonic bomber projects, such as the Convair B-58, the British Avro 730 and the Soviet Myasichev Bounder, either entered service only briefly or were never put in production, since their kind of performance seemed irrelevant in the age of the nuclear missile. The US XB-70 Valkyrie, designed to cruise at 75,000 ft at Mach 3, was cancelled in 1963 and the FB-111, which ostensibly replaced the B-58 in SAC, entered service only in small numbers.

How then did the strategic bomber survive at all? In the 1950s and early 1960s strategic bomber forces were the instruments of deterrence, kept at a state of virtually constant wartime alert. Like Strategic Air Command and the Soviet DA, the British V-bomber force was the elite of the Royal Air Force and the French Force Aérienne Stratégique flying Mirage IVAs was its equivalent. With uncertainties over the technological progress of ICBMs and submarine-launched ballistic missiles, the political prestige of these bomber forces and their obvious efficacy in upholding the nuclear deterrent meant a retreat from such extreme positions as the British Defence White Paper of 1957, which predicted the imminent demise of the manned military aircraft altogether. Also, when high-altitude operations were ruled out, strategic bomber forces learned how to fly low in order to creep under the missile and radar defences. Their aircraft were extensively engineered to take the punishment of low-level operations and special weapons were developed for low-altitude 'stand-off'

delivery. For example, the ambitious British TSR-2 supersonic low-level bomber, cancelled in 1965, featured one of the first examples of terrain-following radar right from the outset of its design.

Large strategic bombers have the slowest rate of change of any type of combat aircraft. They concentrate a large financial investment in a single aircraft, but their big airframes are suited to absorbing engineering changes, new weapons systems and electronic warfare equipment, and keep a modern combat capability in an old airframe. They also have the very useful ability to carry a large, conventional

bomb load over long ranges. In the Vietnam war, for example, B-52s were modified to carry huge tonnages of conventional bombs for the so-called 'arc light' attacks on Viet Cong troop concentrations and, eventually, on the North Vietnamese cities of Hanoi and Haiphong. Right at the end of their front-line career, RAF Vulcan bombers made attacks at extreme range with iron bombs and anti-radiation missiles on Port Stanley airfield in the series of so-called 'Black Buck' raids.

After the successful test of an atomic device in 1949, the Soviet Union tried desperately to get a weapon system into service that had the range to strike its transatlantic rival. The Tu-95 Bear, with its unique combination of swept wings and turboprops, entered service in 1957 and, in spite of being a relatively slow and vulnerable target, caused the United States to devote very large efforts to building a continental anti-bomber defence system. Whereas the Bear remains in small-scale production 30 years on, the pure jet Myasichev M-4 Bison was a relative failure operationally and served only in small numbers. The Tupolev Tu-22M Backfire, which first flew in 1969, remains in significant production, providing a missile-launch platform targeted against NATO's Atlantic sealanes, if not a strategic intercontinental system.

SAC never lost its military preoccupation with supersonic strategic bombers. In the mid-1960s it drew up a requirement for an eventual replacement for the B-52 that would combine the performance of the FB-11 with the range and bomb load of the B-52. After many changes of direction, this Advanced Manned Strategic Aircraft (AMSA) project was eventually to emerge as the B-1B, one of the cornerstones of the Reagan administration's strategic force modernization programme, looked at in detail below. Similarly, just as Soviet strategic air defence is striving to prove that the day of the manned penetrating bomber is really over and the DA has been relegated from a separate command to become a numbered air force, the Soviets are testing a long-range bomber that, it is reported, will be capable of Mach 2·3 at altitude. Independent sources expect at least 100 Blackjack As to be operational by 1990, armed with air-launched cruise missiles. Naval strike will be another important mission, the aircraft possibly turning out to be the true replacement for Soviet Naval Aviation's Bears and Bisons.

Opposite, above: An aircrew member removes safety flags from a B-52G as other crew members climb aboard during an alert.

Opposite, below: Long maintenance manhours are needed to keep the B-52 fleet operational. Some of the SAC pilots who fly them are now younger than the aircraft themselves.

Below: Quick Reaction Alert scramble for a B-52C crew during a full-scale exercise. The chin blisters house the electro-optical viewing system.

After a long and politically controversial development period, the B-1B is due to enter service with Strategic Air Command in the late 1980s.

This B-1B flying testbed has been used for weapons separation tests.

US strategic bomber force

The B-52 force now numbers some 314, supported by small numbers of training and back-up aircraft. Since entering full USAF service in 1955 the B-52 has undergone numerous improvement programmes and changes of mission. One of the reasons for its longevity is the sheer size of the airframe, able to absorb engineering retrofits and new equipment and still keep flying. From the time of the B-52E model onwards, this massive aircraft, originally designed to cruise serenely in the calm of the stratosphere nine miles high, was modified to operate at low altitude, blasting its way to the target through bad weather, rough terrain and nuclear explosions. Some 75 B-52Ds, dating from 1956 and refurbished 20 years later, soldier on as conventional bombers, but will be phased out by the mid-1980s, leaving the G and H models to fly on to the year 2000.

There are currently 16 squadrons of Gs and Hs (two training) with 151 B-52Gs and 90 B-52Hs, of which 28 are normally assigned to a conventional role. This includes maritime reconnaissance, minelaying and acting as a 'Strategic Projection Force' within the Rapid Deployment Joint Task Force (RDJTF). During Exercise 'Bright Star', for example, which saw US forces on manoeuvres in Egypt in 1981, B-52s flew straight from the US east coast, made strikes in the desert and returned, in-flight refuelling on the way. Some 30 B-52s are in active reserve and 223 of all series are in mothballed deep storage. Under continuous improvement programmes, the Gs and Hs have received considerable updating of both offensive and defensive electronic systems, plus electro-optical long-range viewing systems (EVS) and satellite communication facilities (AFSATCOM).

The primary weapon of the B-52 force is the Short-Range Attack Missile or AGM-69A SRAM, of which there are estimated to be 1140 still in the SAC arsenal.

The SRAM was designed to allow the B-52 force to literally blast its way through to targets, rolling up radar and missile sites on the way if necessary. B-52s can carry up to 20 SRAMs externally or on internal rotary launchers and they can fly up to 100 mi. (160 km) following a ballistic trajectory on inertial guidance or using pre-programmed terrain-following manoeuvres, with a nuclear punch equivalent to a Minuteman III warhead. The Mark 28 free-fall nuclear weapon, of which the B-52 can carry eight, has the enormous yield of 25 megatons.

It was clear by the mid-1970s that the B-52 force, in spite of its electronic updates and ability to fly low and deliver SRAMs, would eventually be confounded by the ever-tightening net of Soviet strategic defence. With the parallel technology of the cruise missile developing, work began on reworking a proportion of the venerable bomber force as ALCM carriers, not as penetrating bombers but as launch platforms for long-range missiles. Full-scale ALCM development began in 1978. Funding was sought in the financial year 1983 budget to adapt 64 B-52Gs and Hs to carry the missile and, in Dec. 1982, the first squadron of 14 aircraft became operational at Griffiss AFB, New York. Full operational capability is planned for 1985, when 104 B-52G aircraft will be loaded, each with 12 ALCMs mounted externally. The conversion of 96 B-52Hs, each to carry up to 20 ALCMs is due to begin in 1986.

FB-111A

SAC also currently operates 58 FB-111As, medium-range, high-altitude strategic bomber variants of the F-111 tactical fighter bomber. They can carry up to six SRAMs, six nuclear free-fall bombs or combinations of the two but, on paper at least, cannot reach the Soviet Union from their US bases at Pease AFB, New Hampshire, and Pittsburgh AFB, New York, without refuelling. There have been many proposals to 'stretch' the FB-111, none of which have been put into effect. The nuclear-armed F-111s, based at

Lakenheath and Upper Heyford in the United Kingdom, come under the operational command of US Air Forces Europe.

The aerial tanker force

The Boeing 707 airliner, which ushered in the age of the mass civil jet travel in the 1960s, was based on a military aircraft, the KC-135 flight-refuelling tanker, first flown in 1956. Since then 700 or so KC-135s have been a vital component of US strategic planning and tactical operations worldwide. The aging KC-135 fleet is being re-engined and re-winged, initially with ex-707 turbofan engines bought on the civil market and later with new CFM56 high-bypass turbofans, keeping the aircraft operational beyond the year 2000. The proposal to acquire 44 KC-10 Extenders, tanker transport developments of the DC-10 airliner, has been cut back by Congress.

Bomber force modernization

The ALCM and the follow-on advanced air-launched cruise missile to be built by General Dynamics is the key to US bomber force modernization. Further, all B-52Gs and Hs will be fitted with a new Offensive Avionics System (OAS), and some will be specially hardened against the effects of electromagnetic pulse (EMP) and will receive improved electronic counter-measures equipment. The US Air Force has requested appropriation for a $1 billion programme to produce a common strategic rotary launcher (CSRL) to accommodate ALCMs, SRAMs and free-fall bombs on B-52s, B-1Bs and the so-called 'stealth' bomber. In spite of the huge investment in cruise missiles, the manned penetrating bomber is still central for force modernization plans and, if anything, the resulting B-1B programme has been even more controversial.

When the B-1 bomber, under development from the late 1960s, was cancelled by President Carter in June 1977 the stated reasons were cost, the effectiveness of the ALCM in doing the same job more cheaply and the projected inability of the B-1 to penetrate Soviet air defences. When President Reagan announced plans to build 100 B-1Bs in Oct. 1981 he was fulfilling a long-standing political promise. By the end of the year Congress had approved the plans, after intense lobbying by the manufacturers and by the USAF, who argued that maintaining the B-52 fleet to

An extensive EW fit is designed to increase the B-1B's capacity to survive. This is a mock-up of the offensive and defensive avionics operator's station.

The big Tu-20 Bear D continues in Soviet service and perhaps even in production, 30 years after it first flew. Although no longer a penetrating bomber, it is a very useful platform for maritime reconnaissance and stand-off weapons.

the end of the century would cost as much as the $100 billion bill for a new long-range combat aircraft force. Part of the political debate centred on the allocation of resources between the B-1B and the advanced technology bomber (ATB), the 'stealth' bomber, which, it was envisaged, would enter service in the early 1990s. It was planned that the ATB should then take over the B-1B's role as a manned penetrating bomber, leaving the B-1B to continue as an ALCM carrier and strategic power projection aircraft.

B-1B

Supporters of the B-1 programme state that the USAF needs a manned, penetrating bomber to achieve complete and flexible target coverage of the Soviet Union and, because it can carry all sorts of counter-measures plus, of course, human beings, it can confound and get through defences that the ALCM cannot. Others would point to the role that long-range manned bombers might play in a war in Europe, attacking deep counterair and interdiction targets and operating from secure, remote airfields, in the case where NATO's forward air bases had themselves been destroyed.

There are doubts—and not just about the pro-gramme's huge expense. In the first hearings the Secretary of Defense, Caspar Weinberger, stated that the B-1B would be able to penetrate Soviet air defences until 1990. Then he revised this estimate to 'well into the 1990s'. The B-1B is designed to do this in three ways. It has variable-geometry wings, set

forward for takeoff from runways much shorter than those required for B-52 operation, but swept back for low-level flight at high subsonic speed. Shorter takeoff allows B-1B operations from widely dispersed air-fields, thus increasing the force's 'survivability'. The aircraft can approach its target fast at low level, coming in under the radar, jinking and bucking around hills and valleys, using terrain-following radar.

The B-1B has a radar cross-section of around ten square feet, 0.1% that of a B-52, and the carefully shaped and blended airframe is packed with elec-tronics. The Boeing Military Airplane Company provides the offensive avionics system, which in-cludes forward-looking and terrain-following radar, an extremely accurate inertial navigation system and doppler radar altimeter, plus a highly sophisticated navigation and weapon delivery system. Also on board is AFSATCOM satellite communication equip-ment.

Defensive avionics are built round the AN/ALQ-161 electronic countermeasures system developed by Eaton Corporation's AIL Division, which controls a large number of jamming transmitters and antennae. These generate 'jamming chains' around the periphery of the aircraft to jam signals coming from hostile radars. A separate network of antennae, receivers and processor act as the AN/ALQ-161's 'ears', picking up and identifying new signals and directing jamming operations. On stated USAF figures the AN/ALQ-161 consumes 120 kw of power in an 'all-out' jamming mode. There is also the ALQ-153 tail radar warning receiver and, if all else fails, the ALQ-161 will launch radar-blinding chaff clouds or flares to draw off an attack by heat-seeking missiles.

The differences between the B-1B and the original

B-1, of which four prototypes were built, are hard to distinguish externally. The internal structure will be strengthened to increase the gross takeoff weight from 395,000 lb to 477,000 lb (more than that of the B-52) and the B-1's crew escape capsules have been replaced by ejector seats. The variable-geometry engine inlets, which raised the cost of the B-1 programme so much but allowed Mach 2 speeds, will be replaced by fixed inlets, optimized for the B-1B's low-level, subsonic penetration mission at much lower speeds. The first B-1B is scheduled to fly in 1985 and enter service with SAC in 1986. By 1990 there will be a hundred-strong force.

Long-range aviation

Despite building several large multi-engined, long-range aircraft in the 1930s, the Soviet Union never developed a long-range bomber force during World War II. It is worth noting that at the height of the German conquest, unoccupied Soviet territory was nearly 1000 mi. from Berlin. In the late 1940s the Tupolev design bureau produced a virtual copy of the B-29 called the Tu-4 (known as Bull to NATO) and this was the very first Soviet strategic weapon delivery system. The first Soviet atomic weapon was tested in 1949, very much sooner than Western intelligence had predicted.

Of the two domestic products of the early 1950s, the turboprop-powered Tupolev Tu-95 Bear and the jet-powered Myasichev M-4 Bison, the pre-jet bomber, proved a comparative and embarrassing failure, whereas the old Bear seems to soldier on and on and is apparently still in production. Some 45 Bisons remain configured to carry free-fall bombs and 35 have been adapted as tankers. There are 105 Bear bombers still in service, 70 of them capable of carrying the AS-3 Kangaroo 650-km-range air-to-surface missile.

In 1980 Long Range Aviation (Dal'naya Aviatsiya or DA) disposed of 535 medium-range bombers, 310 aging Tu-16 Badgers and 125 Tu-22 Blinders, operational since the early 1960s, plus 100 of the much more modern Tu-22Ms or Backfire, operational since the mid-1970s. Since then Soviet military aviation has undergone a major organization, with the DA relegated to being a numbered Air Army (36th), with two divisions of Bisons and Badgers. The 46th Air Army, with its headquarters at Smolensk, now operates Badgers, Blinders and Backfires in the European theatre strike role.

A stumbling block in the original SALT talks was the question whether the DA was primarily targeted against the continental United States, although the Soviets argued that the bomber force was not exclusively an intercontinental offensive delivery system. The Backfire's ability to reach the United States with mid-air refuelling became a hotly contested issue, although the unratified treaty eventually contained an exchange of statements to the effect that the Backfire was not to be regarded as a heavy bomber

The Tu-22M Backfire caused a great stir when it was first detected in the west and is a formidable offensive aircraft. This example carries an AS-4 Kitchen ASM under the fuselage.

unless it was armed with long-range cruise missiles. Meanwhile, numbers of Backfires in service both with the DA and with Naval Aviation are increasing significantly. Some will be new aircraft, Backfire-Bs, with an estimated production rate of 42 a year, while others will be older A models rebuilt to -B standard. A new variant (called Backfire-C by NATO), with new engines and revised intake geometry, began to enter service in 1983. The Soviet Navy currently operates 80 Tu-22Ms armed with AS-4 Kingfish air-to-surface missiles, along with more than 300 older Badger and Blinder medium-range bombers.

The Soviet medium bomber force of both the DA and the Navy, with its capabilities now far extended by the Tu-22M/AS-4 combination, has always been a particular concern of UK air defence planners. This has developed into a general concern for the vulnerability of the NATO Atlantic sea route to attack both from below and above the water, with long-range aircraft providing data for over-the-horizon cruise missile attack by submarines.

Although the Soviet Union virtually abandoned heavy bomber development in the 1950s, it did not cease entirely. Production of the very useful long-range Bears still continues at a trickle to replace those lost or worn out, but throughout the 1970s there were persistent hints and intelligence reports of a Soviet bomber that was bigger and more capable even than Backfire. It was first known as Bomber-X in the West, then Ram-P after a satellite photograph revealed a big, variable-geometry aircraft on the apron at the Ramenskoye flight test centre. In 1982 it was given the Department of Defense reporting name, Blackjack. The bomber comes from the Tupolev design bureau and, according to US reports, is 25% bigger than the B-1. It is powered by four new afterburning turbofans mounted in pairs under the fixed section of the wing.

Glossary

AAA Anti-aircraft artillery

AAM air-to-air missile

ACA Agile Combat Aircraft

ADTAC Air Defense Tactical Air Command (US)

AFTI Advanced Fighter Technology Integrator

Ahip Advanced helicopter improvement programme (US Army)

AMRAAM Advanced Medium-Range AS Air-to-Air Missile

All-aspect Missile able to home on target from any direction, not just, for example, in stern chase

ASPJ Advanced Self-Protection Jammer

ASW Anti-Submarine Warfare

ATF Advanced Tactical Fighter

AWACS Airborne Warning and Control System

BMEWS Ballistic Missile Early Warning System

CAP Combat Air Patrol

CAS Close Air Support

CBU Cluster Bomb Unit

CCV Control Configuration Vehicle

CENTCOM US Central Command (South West Asia)

Conformal Design of fuel or weapons stowage to blend with airframe exterior surface

Counterair Military operations designed to attack or protect enemy air power assets

CRAF US Civil Reserve Air Fleet

CTOL Conventional take-off and landing

DARPA Defense Advanced Research Projects Agency (US)

Divad Divisional Air Defence (gun)

Doppler radar Airborne radar which makes use of Doppler effect (frequency shift) in signals reflected from ahead and behind aircraft to give measure of speed over the ground and to distinguish moving targets

Drone remotely piloted air vehicle

Dual Capable System such as aircraft capable of delivering nuclear and/or conventional weapons

ECCM Electronic Counter countermeasures

ECM Electronic Countermeasures

EMP Electro-Magnetic Pulse

EO Electro-Optical

EW Electronic Warfare

FAC Forward Air Controller

FBW Fly-by-Wire

FLIR Forward Looking Infrared

Fire and forget A missile equipped with mid-flight inertial guidance plus active terminal homing or a heat-seeking missile which does not require target illumination or guidance commands from launch aircraft once launched

GCI Ground Control Intercept

GLLD Ground Laser Locator Designator

GPS Global Positioning System

HARM High Speed Anti-Radiation Missile

HUD Head Up Display, cockpit display presenting data in pilot's line of sight

IA-PVO Soviet air defence of the homeland manned interceptor forces

IFF Identification Friend or Foe

INS Inertial navigation system

IR infrared, electromagnetic radiation sensed as heat

JSTARS Joint Surveillance and Target Attack Radar System

JTACMS Joint Tactical Missile System

JTIDS Joint Tactical Information Distribution System

LAMPS Light Airborne Multi-Purpose System (US Navy)

Lantirn Low Altitude Navigation and Target Attack System for Night

LGB Laser-Guided Bomb

LHX Light Helicopter Experimental

LLLTV Low light level television

LRMTS Laser ranger and marked target seeker

MOB Main Operating Base

NOP Nuclear Operation Plan (NATO)

OTH-B Over the Horizon Backscatter (radar)

PAH Panzer Abwehr Hubschrauber Anti-tank helicopter
PVO-Strany Soviet National Air Defence Organization
RAFG Royal Air Force Germany
R & D research and development
RPV Remotely-Piloted Vehicle
RWR Radar warning receiver
SAC Strategic Air Command (USAF)
SACEUR Supreme Allied Commander Europe
SAM Surface-to-Air Missile
SARH Semi-Active Homing,
Semi-active guidance system for missiles using active signals generated elsewhere reflected off the target on which to home
Sea Skimmer anti-ship missile that flies just above wavetops to present the most difficult target to defence systems
Smart Colloquial expression applied to weapon systems which have high degree of on-board autonomous guidance ability, i.e., laser-guided bombs
SRAM Short Range Attack Missile
TAC Tactical Air Command (USAF)
TADS Target Acquisition and Designation System
TARPS Tactical Air Reconnaissance Pd System (US Navy)
TGSM Terminally Guided Sub-Munition
TFR Terrain-Following Radar
TOW Tube-Launched Optically Tracked Wire Guided (anti-tank missile)
USAFE United States Air Force Europe

Acknowledgements

Endpapers Matra, 2-3 McDonnell Douglas, 4-5 British Aerospace, 7 MBB, 8 US Air Force, 11 McDonnell Douglas, 13 (left) MBB (right) US Air Force, 14 MBB, 15 MBB, 17 US Air Force, 18 US Air Force, 19 Dassault-Bréguet, 22 US Air Force, 23 British Aerospace, 26 (top) British Aerospace (below) US Air Force, 27 Dassault-Bréguet, 29 (left) Israeli Aircraft Industries (top right) IAI (below right) Northrop, 30 McDonnell Douglas, 31 (both pictures) US Air Force, 34 General Electric, 35 (top) US Air Force (below) General Electric, 38 (both pictures) US Air Force, 39 US Air Force, 41 (both pictures) Matra, 42-3 British Aerospace, 45 (top) MBB (below) Ferranti, 46-7 Lockheed, 48 General Dynamics, 51 US Air Force, 52-3 MoD, 55 (both pictures) MoD, 56-7 MoD, 58 US Air Force, 59 US Air Force, 60 (top right) US Army (top left) MoD, 60-1 US Air Force, 62 Dassault-Bréguet, 63 (left) Dassault-Bréguet (right) Matra, 64 (top) Ford

Aerospace (below) Martin Marietta, 65 (below) Ford Aerospace, 67 US Army, 68-9 (main picture) McDonnell Douglas (inset) US Air Force, 71 US DoD, 73 (top) US Air Force (below) Novosti, 74 MBB, 76 General Electric, 77 (both pictures) US Army, 78-9 US Army, 80 (top) Hughes Helicopters (below) MBB, 81 US Army, 84 (top) Bell Textron (below) Martin Marietta, 86-7 (all pictures) Hughes Helicopters, 90-1 Boeing Vertol, 92 Sikorsky, 93 Aérospatiale, 94 US Army, 95 McDonnell Douglas, 96 Sikorsky, 97 Bell Textron, 98 Grumman, 100 Grumman, 101 (left) Beechcraft, 102-3 Canadair, 104 Grumman, 106 Grumman, 108 (top) Boeing (bottom) US Air Force, 110-11 US Air Force, 112 Grumman, 113 (both pictures) Lockheed, 114 Grumman, 117 McDonnell Douglas, 118-19 US Navy, 120 US Navy, 121 British Aerospace, 122-3 US Navy, 126-7 MoD (Royal Navy), 128 Aérospatiale, 130-1

McDonnell Douglas, 132 IAI, 133 (both pictures) US Navy, 134-5 (both pictures) MoD (Royal Navy), 136 (top) Aérospatiale (below) MBB, 137 Dassault-Bréguet, 138-9 McDonnell Douglas, 140 US Navy, 141 McDonnell Douglas, 142-3 British Aerospace, 144 Sikorsky, 145 Aérospatiale, 147 Dassault-Bréguet, 148 MoD, 149 (top) Lockheed (below) Dassault-Bréguet, 150 Lockheed, 152 Lockheed, 153 (top) Lockheed (below) US Air Force, 154-5 US Air Force, 156 US Air Force, 157 (top) McDonnell Douglas (below) US Air Force, 158-9 Lockheed, 160-1 (both pictures) US DoD, 162-3 McDonnell Douglas, 164 (top) Aeritalia, (below) Tass, 165 US Air Force, 166 Rockwell International, 168 Boeing, 169 (both pictures) US Air Force, 170-1 US Air Force, 172-3 US Air Force, 174-5 US Air Force, 176-7 (all pictures) US Air Force, 178-9 US Air Force, 180 US Air Force, 181 Boeing, 182 US Navy, 183 US DoD.

Index

Page numbers in italics refer to illustrations